3. 4 card sint, play middl

2 touching suits play low

D0492010

IMPROVE
YOUR BRIDGE

IMPROVE YOUR BRIDGE

RIXI MARKUS

THE BODLEY HEAD
LONDON SYDNEY
TORONTO

British Library Cataloguing
in Publication Data
Markus, Rixi
Improve your bridge.
1. Contract bridge
I. Title
795.4'15   GV1282.3
ISBN 0-370-30192-7

© Rixi Markus 1979
Printed in Great Britain for
The Bodley Head Ltd
9 Bow Street, London WC2E 7AL
by Redwood Burn Ltd
Trowbridge & Esher
Set in Monotype Imprint
by Gloucester Typesetting Co. Ltd
First published 1979

CONTENTS

PREFACE

In this book I am trying to acquaint my readers with some of my own experiences during my bridge career. It is meant for players who have absorbed the essentials and are just beginning to play bridge on a higher level.

The other group of players I would like to reach are those who have played bridge for many years and somehow have stopped progressing. They are either finding the more sophisticated methods too difficult or are quite satisfied with their own performance. The hints offered in *Improve Your Bridge* will show them how to sharpen up their game. They will then give their partners greater satisfaction and learn to understand how much easier and more enjoyable it can be to take the right road to better bridge.

London 1979   RIXI MARKUS

I

The Opening Bid

The Milton Work Point Count system (ace=4, king=3, queen=2, jack=1) is in universal use these days and I expect you all add up your points before deciding whether or not to open the bidding. That is fine; I have always found the point count to be an excellent guide, and I do not know a single expert player who does not use the point count system as a basis for hand evaluation. However, you will find that experts make adjustments for long suits and poor honour holdings—adjustments which are based on their experience and intuition rather than on a rigid set of rules. For example, they will describe a hand as being 'a good 14' or '14 with good shape', instead of attempting to evaluate the distributional strength of the hand in terms of points. If you are anxious to have a set of rules which will almost always lead to the same answer as the expert's personal evaluation, I would suggest that you bear in mind the following:

(a) Add 1 point if you hold all four aces.
(b) Deduct 1 point for an aceless hand, for king singleton, or for queen-jack doubleton.
(c) When thinking of opening the bidding with a suit bid, add 1 point for a doubleton, 2 points for a singleton, and 3 points for a void.

♠ A 7 4 2	♠ 7 5
♡ Q J	♡ A K 7 5 3
♢ Q 9 5	♢ 2
♣ K 8 5 3	♣ K Q 6 4 2
(Hand A)	(Hand B)

Both these hands contain 12 high-card points, but Hand B is clearly much stronger. By applying the adjustment which I suggest, we arrive at the right answer; the first hand becomes 11 points and the second hand 15—counting 1 point for the doubleton and 2 points for the singleton.

I shall be considering the point-count requirements for an opening bid of 1NT in greater detail in Chapter 3. If we assume for the time being that you are playing what is known as a 'weak and strong no trump', that is, 12–14 points not vulnerable and 16–18 points vulnerable, we can go on to consider what you should do when your hand contains 13 points or more but does not qualify for an opening bid of 1NT. The answer is, of course, that you should open one of a suit, but the selection of which suit to open is often of vital importance to the success of the subsequent auction. If you have just one long suit, of course, what to open presents no problem, but you may have to be a little careful if you have two or more suits of equal length, and even if you have just one four-card suit.

♠ A K 7 3
♡ J 9 5
♢ Q 4 2
♣ K 10 7

What to open on this hand depends to some extent on what kind of no trump you decide to play. If your 1NT at the prevailing vulnerability is weak, then you can get the hand off your chest in just one bid. Otherwise, you will have to open one of a suit, and here again the correct opening will depend on your system. Playing the strong no trump as I do, I can open the hand 1♠ and rebid 2NT if partner responds at the two level, for a forced rebid of 2NT shows no more than a minimum opening bid. This is the so-called CAB style of bidding. Playing more normal Acol, however, a rebid of 2NT always shows extra values, and the sequence 1♠–2♣–2NT would guarantee 15–16 points. This means that, if you are playing Acol and a strong no trump, you will have to open 1♣ on this hand; this is almost the only case where it is correct to open with a three-card suit.

Notice that, when considering what to open on the above hand, we had to think about what we were going to bid if partner made an awkward response in clubs or diamonds. This principle, which I call the Principle of Preparedness, is a very important one, and it is one which must always be borne in mind when you are contemplating your opening bid—the question you must ask yourself is, 'Have I a convenient rebid no matter what partner might respond?'

♠ 7 2
♥ A K J 8
♦ Q 6 3
♣ K 10 6 5

This hand contains 14 points, including 1 point for the doubleton spade, and it is clearly worth an opening bid. Which suit would you open? It would be pleasant to be able to open with the excellent heart suit, but you must always bear in mind what you are going to rebid on the second round. To open 1♥ would leave you with an awkward rebid after a 2♦ response from your partner: all you could possibly do would be to raise to 3♦, but this would be misleading on such a balanced hand and on such minimum values. The correct opening is, in fact, 1♣, for this leaves you prepared for any possible response—you can bid 1♥ over 1♦, raise 1♥ to 2♥, or bid 1NT over 1♠. Remember, too, that even if you were playing the weak no trump, 1NT would be a poor bid on this hand: with a small doubleton in one suit and 11 of your 13 high-card points concentrated in just two suits, you should always open with a suit bid if it is at all possible.

This same Principle of Preparedness applies when you have two 'touching' suits.

♠ 7 3
♥ A J 10 4
♦ A K J 7
♣ J 5 3

Diamonds is by far the best suit on this hand, but to open 1♦ would leave you with an impossible rebid over 1♦–2♣. To bid 2♥ at that point would be a reverse bid, showing a stronger hand and guaranteeing longer diamonds than hearts, and to bid anything else would be equally misleading. The answer clearly is to open 1♡ on the hand, intending to rebid 2◇ over 2♣ and, if you prefer it, 1NT over 1♠.

The rule with two 'touching' suits (spades and hearts, hearts and diamonds, or diamonds and clubs) is simple: open with the higher-ranking four-card suit first.

The most difficult hand on which to find the correct opening bid is one containing four spades and four diamonds, but here again the Principle of Preparedness will give us the right answer.

♠ A Q 8 3
♡ K 8 4
◇ K J 9 7
♣ 10 5

The prepared opening bid here is 1♠, intending to bid 2◇ over 2♣ and to raise a response of 2♡ (which guarantees a five-card suit) to 3♡. To open 1◇ on this hand would leave you in an impossible situation if partner were to respond 2♣.

♠ A Q 8 3
♡ 10 5
◇ K J 9 7
♣ K 8 4

This is the same hand with the clubs and hearts reversed. The result is that an opening bid of 1♠ is now out of the question: that is, unless your system (like mine) permits a rebid of 2NT over 2♡. Playing normal Acol methods, an opening bid of 1◇ is preferable, for you can at least raise a response of 2♣ to 3♣. However, even this is not completely satisfactory, and my own view is that there is a strong case for opening this awkward hand with the slightly unusual bid of 1♣.

To summarize, with four spades and four diamonds, open 1NT whenever possible; otherwise, open 1♠ if you also hold three hearts or if you are strong enough to rebid 2NT; open 1◇, or possibly 1♣, on all other hands.

If you hold *three* four-card suits, you will find it easiest to locate any available fit if you open the suit below the singleton, the suit below clubs for this purpose being spades.

♠ A J 9 5
♡ 7
♢ A K 8 2
♣ K 10 7 5

Open 1♢, the suit below the singleton. If partner responds 1♠ or 2♣, your problems are over; and if he makes the more likely response of 1♡, you can continue the search for a playable fit by rebidding 1♠.

The only exception to this general rule occurs when your three four-card suits are 'touching'.

♠ 7
♡ J 9 6 3
♢ A K 10 4
♣ K Q 9 8

Open 1♢. When one of the three touching suits is very poor, it is best to ignore it and be content to show the other two suits; this heart suit is not worth mentioning unless partner can introduce it from his side of the table.

So much for *what* to open; we must now move on to consider the question of *when* to open the bidding. As I mentioned earlier, all 13-point hands qualify for an opening bid, and some 12-point hands are well worth opening. In doubtful cases, one deciding factor should be whether or not you have a good suit, with a good proportion of your high-card points concentrated in the suit or suits which you are planning to bid.

♠ 9 5	♠ K 7 2
♡ A K 10 9 5	♡ J 8 6 4 3
♢ K 7 2	♢ J 8 3
♣ J 8 3	♣ A Q
(Hand A)	(Hand B)

Both these hands contain 12 points, counting 1 point for the doubleton, but only Hand A warrants an opening bid of 1♡; I wouldn't dream of opening 1♡ on Hand B, in view of the very ragged suit and the concentration of points in the short suits, where they are of less value.

Other important factors to bear in mind when you are deciding whether or not to open on shaded values are the vulnerability and your position at the table. You should make every effort to open the bidding when you are the dealer, for in so doing you might make life awkward for either opponent—or even for both opponents. Second in hand openings, on the other hand, should always be well up to standard: once one opponent has passed, there is an even-money chance whether it is partner or the other opponent who has the majority of the missing strength, and a flimsy opening bid is just as likely to mislead partner as it is to unsettle your left-hand opponent. The ideal position for a light opening bid is, of course, third in hand, when you can be almost certain that the opponent on your left has fair values. However, it is a common mistake to open light third in hand just for the sake of it; this is pointless, and it is important to make sure that a thin opening bid is likely to do some good before you venture an opening on 10 or 11 points. This means two things: try to open a major suit, which is going to have some pre-emptive effect, and try to open a good suit, so that you at least indicate the correct opening lead to your partner if the opponents eventually play the hand.

♠ A 5 2		♠ K Q J 8 5	
♡ J 8 3		♡ 5 2	
◇ K 2		◇ K 8 3	
♣ Q 7 4 3 2		♣ 10 7 5	
(Hand A)		(Hand B)	

Hand A actually contains more points than Hand B, but 1♣ would be a very bad opening, even third in hand. However, there is a lot to be said for a third in hand opening of 1♠ on Hand B: it is always difficult for the opponents to bid over the spade suit, and you will certainly welcome a spade lead from your partner if the person on your left eventually becomes the declarer.

2

The First Response
to One of a Suit

The simplest response which you can make after partner has opened the bidding with one of a suit is an immediate limit raise in his suit. Several different methods have been devised to aid the responder in evaluating his hand for this purpose; none of these is completely satisfactory but, for those of you who like to be able to count points in every situation, I would suggest that you should make the following additions to the usual point count to allow for the distribution of your hand.

Assuming you have at least four of partner's suit:

> Add 1 point for a doubleton
> Add 3 points for a singleton
> Add 5 points for a void.

Having made these adjustments, raise to two with 5–9 points, to three with 10–11 points, and to four with 12 points or more.

> ♠ Q J 9 3
> ♡ K Q 7 4 3
> ◇ 2
> ♣ 10 5 2

If partner opens 1♡ or 1♠, this hand becomes worth 11 points, counting 3 points for the singleton diamond; it is therefore well worth a direct raise to three.

If partner has opened with one of a major suit, you should *always* give an immediate raise to the appropriate level if you have four-card trump support; the only exception to this occurs if you are too strong to limit your hand immediately, in which case it may be necessary to make a forcing take-out in another suit or, if you are slightly weaker, to make what is known as a Delayed Game Raise.

♠ A Q 7 3
♡ Q 2
◇ 9 5
♣ A Q 10 7 3

Opposite an opening bid of 1♠, this hand is too strong for an immediate jump to 4♠. Such action might well result in a slam being missed, and the recommended way of dealing with this kind of hand is to respond 2♣ and then, if partner rebids 2◇, 2♡, 2NT or 3♣, jump to 4♠ on the second round; this will show a good club suit and a hand which was just too good for a direct raise to game.

If, on the other hand, partner's opening bid is 1♣ or 1◇, it is no longer imperative to give an immediate limit raise; in fact, it is often correct to make an exploratory bid in a new suit even if you have four-card support for partner's suit.

♠ K 10 7 5 3
♡ 7 2
◇ Q 10 4 2
♣ A 5

If your partner opens 1◇, this hand obviously contains the values for a raise to 3◇; however, it is quite possible that the best game contract might be in spades or even in no trumps, and the correct response is 1♠—intending to show the diamond support later if the occasion arises.

To raise partner's suit to the three or four level guarantees at least four-card support. Some players like to insist that a raise to two should also show four trumps, but my view is that such a rigid set of rules is quite impractical. Quite often an immediate raise on three trumps is by far the best response.

♠ K 7 2
♡ 2
◇ Q 9 7 5 3
♣ J 8 4 2

Opposite an opening bid of 1♠, it is difficult to see what else you can possibly do but bid 2♠. The hand is far too weak to bid

2♢ and far too strong to pass, and to bid 1NT on such a hand would be a dreadful distortion.

Another situation in which it is correct to raise on three trumps occurs when the opponents enter the auction. Consider the following hand:

> ♠ K 7 5 3
> ♡ Q 8 2
> ♢ 7 5
> ♣ K 10 4 3

If partner opens 1♡, you have an obvious response of 1♠— that is, until your right-hand opponent comes in with 2♢. The hand is clearly not worth a bid of 2♠ at this point, for this would force partner to rebid at the three level; once again a raise to 2♡ is the only possible bid.

So much for hands on which you are in the happy position of being able to raise partner's suit. Unfortunately, things may not always be so straightforward and, more often than not, you will not have primary support for the suit which partner has opened. In that case, assuming that you have the values to make a bid of any kind, you will have to continue to search for a playable fit by introducing a new suit. If you have more than one biddable suit, the rules governing which one to bid first are quite straight-forward, as follows.

Whenever possible, respond in your longest suit first. The only exception to this general rule occurs when your long suit is lower-ranking than partner's and your hand is not strong enough to bid at the two level.

> ♠ Q 7 3 2
> ♡ 9 8
> ♢ K J 10 6 3
> ♣ J 7

If partner opens 1♣, the correct response is obviously 1♢. However, now suppose that partner opens 1♡. To bid a new suit at the two level guarantees at least 9 high-card points, and this means that a response of 2♢ is out of the question; even though the diamond suit is both longer and stronger, therefore, the correct response to 1♡ is 1♠.

When you have two or more four-card suits, the rule is to bid them 'upwards'—that is, to bid the cheapest one first. This applies no matter how strong the respective suits are.

♠ K Q J 9
♡ Q 7 5 4
◇ 7 2
♣ 9 7 3

If partner opens 1♣ or 1◇, bid 1♡—even though the spades are so much stronger. If partner has a spade suit he will, of course, bid it over 1♡, and there is therefore no danger of missing a spade fit. A response of 1♠, on the other hand, would run the risk of bypassing a 4–4 heart fit; for example, suppose the full hands are something like:

West	East
♠ A 2	♠ K Q J 9
♡ A J 8 2	♡ Q 7 5 4
◇ 10 5 3	◇ 7 2
♣ K Q 8 4	♣ 9 7 3

A quiet part-score in hearts should produce nine tricks on this hand, but, if East responds 1♠ to 1♣, he is in danger of having to watch his partner incur a minus score in 1NT.

This principle of bidding four-card suits in ascending order does, of course, mean that your selection of the suit in which to respond may vary according to partner's opening bid.

♠ 6 5
♡ K Q 8 3
◇ 10 9 7
♣ A J 6 3

If partner opens 1◇, you have an obvious response of 1♡; if, on the other hand, he opens 1♠, the correct bid is 2♣—not 2♡. In fact, there is a very important point to bear in mind here: because of the enormous amount of bidding space it eats up, it is generally agreed that a response of 2♡ to 1♠ should guarantee at least a five-card suit; this leaves the opener free to raise with three-card support and may well relieve him of a difficult rebid problem.

Your choice of response may also be affected by the intervention of the opponents.

♠ K 10 8 4
♡ A 2
♢ Q J 9 3
♣ 7 5 4

If partner opens 1♡, your correct response is obviously 1♠. However, now suppose that your right-hand opponent comes in with an overcall of 2♣ over 1♡: spades is no longer the cheapest suit in which to respond, and your best bid now is 2♢; this leaves more room for partner to manoeuvre. Another important point to remember in this connection is that any bid like 2♠ in this sequence (that is, a bid at the two level in a higher-ranking suit than partner's) must show fair values and must guarantee at least a five-card suit. The fact that the bidding has been pushed up in this way may leave partner with a difficult rebid problem, and it may well make life easier for him if he is able to raise on three-card support.

Unless the responder has previously passed, a simple response in a new suit is, of course, completely forcing, and the opener has to find at least one more bid. This means that it is safe to make a simple waiting move on any number of points, and the range of the change of suit response is a very wide one—from 5 to 15 points. With more than 15 points, it is usual to make a forcing take-out in a new suit. Such a jump is forcing to game, and it may be the vital first move in reaching a slam if the opener also has something in reserve.

It is, of course, possible to make a forcing take-out on fewer than 16 points, and this will often be the correct action when you have an excellent fit for partner's suit.

♠ K Q 10 5
♡ 9 4
♢ 7 3
♣ A K Q 10 4

This hand is well worth a jump to 3♣ if partner opens 1♠; with such a good fit and such a powerful club suit, partner must be alerted to the possibility of a slam as soon as possible. If partner's opening bid were 1♢ or 1♡, on the other hand, a simple response of 2♣ would be quite enough for the time being.

Another situation in which it is best to make a forcing take-out on minimum high-card values is where you have a very good, self-supporting suit of your own.

> ♠ 10 8
> ♡ A K Q 10 9 7
> ♢ 5 3
> ♣ A 7 4

If partner opens 1♣ or 1♢, bid 2♡ and rebid hearts at every subsequent opportunity. If you make a simple response of 1♡ on this hand, you will find yourself with a tricky bidding problem on the next round and you will have great difficulty in convincing partner that you have such a powerful hand and such a powerful suit.

The only kind of response which remains to be considered when partner has opened with one of a suit is that of a number of no trumps. An immediate response of 2NT or 3NT is completely natural, showing a balanced hand with 11–12 or 13–15 points respectively. A response of 1NT is also natural and non-forcing, showing 5–9 points, but there are situations in which you may have to bid 1NT on a hand which is far from balanced.

> ♠ 7 5
> ♡ 3 2
> ♢ A Q 9 2
> ♣ J 10 7 5 4

If partner opens 1♡ or 1♠, you are not strong enough to bid 2♣; as I mentioned earlier, a response in a new suit at the two level guarantees at least 9 points. However, you are too strong to pass, for there is no reason why partner should not have opened with a one bid on 18 or 19 points, and the only possible response is therefore 1NT.

It is possible to take this principle even further.

♠ 2
♥ A 8 7 5 3 2
♦ 10 9 6 3
♣ Q 4

There is no problem if partner opens 1♣ or 1♦, but what would you do if partner opens 1♠? This hand is clearly too weak for a response of 2♥, and once again 1NT is the best bid available: it can hardly be a worse contract than 1♠, and the bidding might well develop in such a way that you can introduce the heart suit at a later stage.

I have already mentioned the way in which an intervening overcall can influence your choice of response to partner's opening bid. There is, of course, another very important weapon in the responder's armoury when the opponents enter the auction: the penalty double. In my view, penalty doubles are one of the biggest money-spinners at rubber bridge, and one of the main attributes which distinguish the good player from the average player is the ability to make a penalty double at the right time.

A double at the four or five level is largely a matter of common sense, taking into account the strength and distribution which partner has shown in the earlier bidding. A penalty double of a low-level contract, on the other hand, is much more difficult to judge correctly. The ideal ingredients for a successful double at the one or two level are surprising length in the opponent's suit and shortage in partner's suit. Consider these two hands:

♠ Q 10 7	♠ 7
♥ K Q 7 5	♥ 10 8 2
♦ A Q 6	♦ Q 10 8 6
♣ 10 5 4	♣ A K 7 5 2
(Hand A)	(Hand B)

Hand A is by far the stronger in terms of high-card points, but Hand B is much better suited to a penalty double if partner opens 1♠ and your right-hand opponent creeps in with 2♦. For one thing, the high-card strength of Hand A makes it quite likely that you will score better by bidding and making a game in spades, hearts or no trumps; your opponent knew he was missing all these high cards when he decided to enter the arena and, since your hand contains no nasty surprises for the overcaller, it is much better suited for playing a contract your way. Hand B, however, is quite different. Your shortage of points and your lack of support for partner's suit make it much less likely that your side can make a game contract. Furthermore, a double of 2◇ should prove quite profitable: you know that the declarer is going to run into an unpleasant trump break, something which he certainly did not take into account when he was deciding whether or not to overcall, and the fact that you have a singleton spade makes it likely that partner's top cards in his long suit will pull their full weight in the defence.

Finally, no discussion of the action which you should take when the opponents overcall the opening bid would be complete without considering the most common intervention of all—the take-out double. My style of bidding when my right-hand opponent makes a take-out double is quite simple and straight-forward: as far as possible, I like to ignore the double completely.

Having said that, of course, I realize that it is impossible to bid completely naturally in the face of a double by the enemy, and there are, in fact, two conventional bids which I find extremely useful in these situations. The first is a redouble, which shows at least 9 points *and* a vague interest in making a penalty double of the opponents' final resting place.

♠ K J 7 5
♡ 8 6
◇ A 6
♣ Q 10 8 4 3

If the bidding starts 1♡-double, this is an ideal hand on which to redouble. You can deal effectively with an escape into one of the black suits by the opponents, and the knowledge that you have values of this kind might enable partner to punish them if they run into diamonds.

I strongly recommend that a redouble should show a desire to penalize the opponents as well as showing that your side has the balance of the points. To my mind, there is no point whatsoever in redoubling if the auction commences 1◇-double and you hold something like:

♠ A K J 9 6 3
♡ 7 2
◇ 9 7
♣ J 8 4

Here you have no desire at all to double the opponents at a low level, and this hand is best described by an immediate jump to 2♠: such a jump cannot possibly have its normal meaning after a take-out double, and I like to play it as non-forcing, showing a good six-card suit and 9 or 10 points.

The second conventional bid which I favour after an opposing double is a jump to 2NT. This bid clearly now has little use in its normal sense, for you would almost certainly prefer to redouble if you held a balanced hand with 11 or 12 points, and it is best used in a conventional sense to show a good raise to three in the opener's suit. This leaves a direct raise to three as a purely pre-emptive bid, showing a hand with long trumps and very few high cards.

♠ 7 6 5
♡ Q 10 7 4 2
◇ 9
♣ J 9 5 3

After 1♡ from partner and a double on your right, make things awkward for the enemy by jumping to 3♡. Partner will know that you have a hand of this kind, for you would bid 2NT over the double if you had a normal constructive raise to 3♡.

One final point about dealing with a take-out double. I have found it extremely effective to bid 1NT as often as possible over the double, even on hands on which I would normally prefer to make an alternative bid; this is because 1NT makes it impossible for the player on your left to bid at the one level, and the opponents might therefore miss an opportunity of competing to their advantage.

♠ Q 3
♡ Q 9 5 3
◇ 8 4 2
♣ K 10 7 4

After 1◇-double, there is a strong case for bidding 1NT on this hand: to make the more normal 1♡ response might enable the opponents to find a spade fit.

3

No Trump Bidding

As I mentioned in the first chapter, the 4–3–2–1 point count system which most of you use works best when you are evaluating your hand for no trump purposes. It is generally agreed that, even if both the hands are balanced, a total of 25 points in the two hands will produce a reasonable play for nine tricks in no trumps. When counting your points with a view to opening with 1NT or 2NT, of course, you should not make any adjustment for short suits, for a doubleton or singleton is certainly of no advantage in a no trump contract. The only adjustments which you should make to the normal high card count are, in fact, to deduct 1 point for poor honour holdings like queen-jack doubleton, and to add 1 point if your hand contains a number of tens and other good intermediate cards.

♠ A 10 9
♡ Q 10 8 3
◇ K 9 8 2
♣ A 10

This hand only contains 13 high-card points, but the powerful intermediates will make it as effective as most 14- or 15-point hands in a no trump contract.

If your hand is reasonably balanced, that is to say, its distribution is either 4–3–3–3 or 4–4–3–2, the most accurate and descriptive opening bid will often be 1NT. It has been found most efficient in practice to play a three-point range for the bid, and I expect you will all have decided already the particular range which you favour. I personally like to play a strong no trump all the time, but some of you will prefer to play what is called 'weak and strong' (that is, 12–14 not vulnerable and 16–18 vulnerable), and the really brave among you may opt for a weak no trump throughout. I have no wish to influence your selection in any way for, while I have found that a strong no trump is both safe and efficient, there is obviously a lot to be said for the pre-emptive effect of a weak no trump, particularly at pairs duplicate. In fact, I am a great believer in allowing my partner to make the choice in these matters: this will help to keep him happy, and putting partner in a good frame of mind at the beginning of the rubber might well be worth a few hundred points in the long run. Just one word of warning about the weak no trump: it is much easier to double a 12–14 1NT than it is to double a strong no trump, so think twice before playing a weak no trump at teams scoring or for money; for one thing, your partner may not play the hands as well as you do.

Whatever strength you choose to allot to your opening 1NT, there are a couple of important points to bear in mind when you are considering your opening bid.

♠ 5 4
♡ K 7 5
◇ A K 5 3
♣ K 5 4 2

Even if you are playing a weak no trump, 1NT would be a poor bid on this hand. The small doubleton spade and the poor intermediate cards make the hand unsuitable for no trump play, and an opening bid of 1◇ will probably work out much better; after all, you can always rebid 1NT if partner covers your poor holding in spades by responding 1♠.

Similarly, try to avoid opening 1NT when the vast majority of your points are concentrated in two suits.

♠ A Q J 4
♡ 7 3 2
◇ J 5
♣ A Q 10 5

Even if this hand falls into your range for an opening bid of 1NT, 1♣ is a much better bid: as 13 of your 14 points are packed into two suits, the best way of describing this hand is to open 1♣ and rebid 1♠ if partner responds in one of the red suits.

An opening bid of 2NT shows a balanced hand, 20–22 points and, ideally, a guard in every suit. Whereas it is never wise to open 1NT with a five-card major suit, an opening bid of 2NT has to cover a wider variety of hands and may well conceal a good holding in hearts or spades.

♠ A K Q 10 4
♥ K 7
♦ A Q 8
♣ K 9 3

This is a difficult hand to manage in any system, but the most practical opening bid is undoubtedly 2NT. To open a mere 1♠ would risk missing a good game contract if partner passes, and the obvious disadvantage of opening with the forcing bid of 2♠ is that, if partner has to make the likely negative response of 2NT, an eventual no trump contract will be played from the wrong side of the table.

More powerful balanced hands are shown by opening with the artificial strength-showing bid of 2♣ and rebidding in no trumps at the first opportunity. To open 2♣ and rebid 2NT shows 23–24 points, and this is in fact the only sequence in which the auction can die short of game after an opening bid of 2♣. If you are lucky enough to hold 25 or 26 points and a balanced hand, open 2♣ and rebid 3NT if partner makes the negative response of 2♦.

♠ A Q
♥ K Q J 7
♦ A K 10 5
♣ K J 9

This hand is slightly too strong for an opening bid of 2NT; the correct way to show it is to open with the forcing bid of 2♣ and, if partner makes the almost inevitable response of 2♦, rebid a non-forcing 2NT.

So much for the balanced hands containing 20 or more points. What if you hold a balanced hand in the 12–19 point-count range and yet you are unable to open the bidding with 1NT? The answer is that you have to open with one of a suit and rebid the appropriate number of no trumps on the next round, and I will now discuss the various no trump rebids in more detail.

Opinions vary among experts about the precise meaning of a rebid of 1NT. There is a well-supported school of thought which suggests that a 1NT rebid should promise the strength which could not have been shown by an opening bid of 1NT: that is to say, the 1NT rebid shows 15–16 points if you are playing a weak no trump, and 12–14 points if your opening 1NT would have been strong. This method has the advantage of being arithmetically tidy, but it makes certain hands extremely difficult to bid accurately.

♠ 6 4
♡ K Q 10
◇ A 9 7 5 3
♣ Q J 8

The most sensible way of describing this hand would seem to be to open 1◇ and rebid 1NT over the likely response of 1♠, but this will no longer be possible if you are playing the weak no trump and your rebid promises a stronger hand. You are therefore left with the unpleasant alternative of opening 1NT, which would be extremely misleading, or opening 1◇ and rebidding 2◇ on the second round, which would considerably overstate the strength of the suit. It is because of this type of hand, which is after all fairly common, that I prefer to keep the 1NT rebid as a flexible bid, showing any hand in the 12–16 point range on which a minimum rebid in no trumps seems to be the best action; this is, in fact, a good example of my general philosophy of bidding—I like to bid what I think I can make.

The strength of a rebid of 2NT depends partly on the system you are playing and partly on the level of partner's first response. A *jump* to 2NT always shows 17–18 points, with a guard in both the unbid suits.

♠ Q 4
♡ A Q 8 7 2
◇ K J 4
♣ A J 9

If partner responds 1♠ to your opening bid of 1♡, the best rebid on this hand is 2NT, which can be passed. Don't worry about concealing the five-card heart suit at this stage: if partner has the values for game and three-card heart support, he can always bid 3♡ over 2NT; this sequence is forcing, and it offers the opener a choice of game contract.

A non-jump rebid of 2NT shows the same 17–18 points if partner's first response was either 1NT or a simple raise of your original suit.

    ♠ K 10 4
    ♡ A Q 9 2
    ◇ K 8 7 5
    ♣ A Q

If you open 1♡ and partner raises to 2♡, the correct rebid on this hand is 2NT. This shows a balanced hand with 17–18 points and suggests that your 1♡ bid was based on a four-card suit; partner should therefore now be in a good position to judge the correct final contract.

It is when partner's first response was a new suit at the two level that opinions vary on the interpretation of a rebid of 2NT. Playing the CAB system and the strong no trump as I do, I prefer a sequence like 1♡–2♣–2NT to show no more than a minimum opening bid. In Acol, however, a 2NT rebid *always* promises extra values, and the above sequence would show 15–16 points.

    ♠ K J 8
    ♡ A J 7 5 2
    ◇ A Q 9
    ♣ 10 7

After 1♡–2♣, the best rebid on this hand in Acol is 2NT. Once again there is no need to worry about missing the best game in a 5–3 heart fit, for partner can always bid a forcing 3♡ over 2NT if he has game-going values and three-card heart support.

The strength required for a jump rebid of 3NT also varies according to partner's initial response. If his first move was to bid 1NT, to raise your original suit to two, or to bid a new suit at the one level, 3NT shows 19 or more points. If, on the other hand, he responded in a new suit at the two level, thereby promising at least 9 points, the requirements for a 3NT rebid can be reduced to 17 points.

♠ A Q
♡ K Q 7 3 2
♢ A 10 5
♣ K J 2

If you open 1♡ and partner responds 1♠, the most descriptive rebid on this hand is 3NT. If, however, partner bids 2♣ over 1♡, you are slightly too strong for a jump to 3NT, which might easily miss a slam in either clubs, hearts or no trumps. The best rebid on this awkward hand is a jump to 3♢, which is forcing to game and which gives partner an opportunity of describing his hand in a little more detail before you decide on the correct final contract.

So far, the opponents have remained obligingly silent when we have been considering no trump rebids by the opener. In real life, of course, they will not always be so considerate, and at this stage one or two important points about no trump bidding in the face of intervention need to be made.

If the opponents' overcall has not had the effect of raising the level of the bidding, all no trump rebids by the opener retain their normal meaning. The only exception to this general rule occurs when the bidding has remained at the one level. Suppose, for example, that you open 1♢ on the following hand, and that your partner responds 1♡.

♠ Q 7 2
♡ 8 3
♢ A Q 10 6
♣ A 9 7 4

You would normally rebid 1NT on this hand, but if your right-hand opponent comes in with 1♠ over 1♡, the correct action is to pass: whatever the strength of your normal 1NT rebid, it should always show more than minimum values if it is made in a voluntary situation of this kind.

If the opponents' antics have had the effect of pushing the bidding up to unpleasant heights, a strong-sounding no trump rebid may in fact hide a weakish hand.

♠ A Q 4
♡ 7 3
◇ K 10 8 5 4
♣ A 9 3

Suppose that you open 1◇ and that your left-hand opponent makes life awkward by overcalling 1♠. If partner now bids 2♡, the only sensible rebid on this hand is 2NT. Partner should not interpret this as showing extra values in this sequence: you are merely saying that you have a minimum hand on which you would have rebid 1NT if the auction had been allowed to proceed 1◇–1♡ in a clear run. This means, of course, that you must be careful if you hold a slightly stronger hand in the same situation.

♠ A Q 4
♡ 7 3
◇ K 10 8 5 4
♣ A K 9

If the bidding once again starts 1◇–1♠–2♡–No Bid, you must jump to 3NT on this hand. When you come to think of it, this should be perfectly safe, for partner must have a goodish hand to force the bidding up in this way.

4

The First Response
to One No Trump

Generally speaking, your first response after partner has opened the bidding with 1 NT will be quite straightforward. I shall just run through the main points before going on to consider the more difficult situations which arise when the player on your right either overcalls or doubles the opening bid.

Whether partner's opening bid of 1 NT is weak or strong does not matter at this stage, for the structure of your responses will be identical in either case: all that varies, of course, is the strength required for the constructive responses. For the sake of simplicity, I shall assume that the 1 NT opening is strong, showing 16–18 points; if your methods favour a 12–14 1 NT, you will just have to make a four-point adjustment from time to time.

The meaning of the various two-level responses to 1 NT is fairly standard, and nearly everybody uses the same methods. 2♦, 2♡ and 2♠ are all weak bids, showing a five-card or longer suit and a hand on which there is no possibility of making a game contract; the opener is expected to pass. A response of 2♣, on the other hand, is hardly ever used as a weakness take-out: it is usually interpreted as Stayman, a conventional bid enquiring about the opener's major suit holdings. Over the 2♣ enquiry, the opener bids a four-card major suit if he has one; otherwise he bids 2♦.

I am not a great believer in playing a large number of artificial conventions, but it seems to me that some kind of Stayman convention is vital over 1 NT.

West	East
♠ A J 5 4	♠ K Q 8 6
♡ A 10 3	♡ 7 2
♦ K Q 7 2	♦ J 6 3
♣ K 8	♣ A 10 7 5

West has a perfectly normal opening bid of 1NT and East clearly has the values for game. However, you will see from the two hands that 3NT would be in grave jeopardy after an opening heart lead and that 4♠ is by far the safer contract—and yet it is difficult to see how the partnership is going to reach a spade contract if they are playing completely natural methods. East clearly cannot respond 2♠, which would be a weakness take-out, and a response of 3♠ would guarantee at least a five-card suit; the only real solution is for him to bid 2♣ (Stayman), and a full auction will proceed 1NT–2♣–2♠–4♠.

Just one word of warning about Stayman: unless the responder has a five-card major suit, he must not use the convention on hands which are too weak for a quantitative raise to 2NT.

♠ Q 10 7 5
♡ K 8 6 3
♢ 7
♣ 9 8 5 2

If you hold this hand and hear your partner open 1NT, it would be pleasant to bid 2♣ and find a 4–4 major suit fit. However, to use Stayman on this hand would be most unwise, for you will be completely stuck if partner is forced to respond 2♢; don't forget that a return to 2NT at this point would be a natural raise, showing 7 or 8 points and inviting partner to go on to three if he has anything to spare. Therefore it is much safer to pass.

If you transform one of those small clubs into a small spade, of course, the situation is completely different, and a Stayman 2♣ enquiry is now the ideal response.

♠ Q 10 7 5 2
♡ K 8 6 3
♢ 7
♣ 9 8 5

If partner replies 2♡ or 2♠, all is well and he will be playing in the best part-score; and if the worst comes to the worst and he bids 2◇, you can still revert to 2♠ and be certain of playing the hand in a reasonable spot.

A jump to three of a suit after partner has opened 1NT is forcing showing a five-card or longer suit. A response of 3♡ or 3♠ is used primarily to give the opener a choice of game contract: if he has three-card support for the responder's suit, he will normally prefer to play in four of the major.

♠ K Q 7 5 2
♡ 8 4
◇ A 10 8 3
♣ J 7

If partner opens 1NT and you hold this hand, don't make the common mistake of introducing a Stayman 2♣. It is not a *four*-card spade suit which you need to find in partner's hand: three-card support will almost certainly be enough to make 4♠ the best game contract, and the correct response is therefore an immediate jump to 3♠.

If the opener has a maximum hand for his opening bid and good support for partner's major suit, he shouldn't just make a sleepy raise to four; he can show that he has an ideal hand by cue-bidding 4♣ or 4◇, and this may make it easier to reach a slam if the responder also has something in reserve.

West
♠ A 10 7 4
♡ K Q 5
◇ K 7
♣ A Q 6 4

East
♠ K Q 8 5 2
♡ 9 7 4
◇ A 8 4
♣ K 5

West opens 1NT and East makes the forcing response of 3♠. West can now bid 4♣ to show good support for spades, a maximum hand, and the ace of clubs—all in one bid. If East had nothing to spare, he could simply return to 4♠ at this point and no harm would be done. As it is, of course, he also has sufficient values to co-operate in the search for a slam, and he can show this by making a cue bid of 4◇. This is obviously all West wants to hear, and nothing should now keep the partnership out of the excellent slam.

An immediate response of 3♣ or 3♢ after 1NT is also strong and forcing; in fact, the implication is that the responder is even stronger than he would need to be for a jump to three of a major, for there would be little point in his showing a long minor suit unless he has some vague hopes of a slam.

♠ Q 7 2
♡ 10 4
♢ A K J 6 3
♣ 8 7 5

If partner opens 1NT, there is no point in showing this excellent diamond suit. Nine tricks in no trumps will almost certainly be easier to make than eleven tricks in diamonds, and you need not look beyond a simple raise to 3NT.

The only other response to 1NT which remains to be considered is an immediate jump to 4♡ or 4♠; this shows a six-card suit and a hand on which the responder has no slam ambitions.

♠ K J 9 7 5 3
♡ 10 6 2
♢ 3 2
♣ K 8

This hand is about right for a direct jump to 4♠ over 1NT. However, if we make the hand slightly stronger, say by replacing the 10 of hearts by the ace, there must be a good chance of making a slam if the opener has a suitable hand opposite. We can therefore no longer content ourselves with a simple bid of 4♠; the correct action now is to bid 3♠, intending to follow with 4♠ if partner bids 3NT: this will suggest a hand of this kind, and the opener will not pass if he has a suitable hand for slam purposes.

So far, the opponents have remained obediently silent over partner's opening bid of 1NT. They will not always be so subdued, however, particularly if you are playing the weak no trump, and we must now think about what happens if your right-hand opponent enters the auction.

If he doubles 1NT, your actions are quite straightforward. If you are fairly sure that partner can make the contract and think you can deal with anything the opponents escape into, you redouble. If you have a weak hand with a five-card or longer suit, you take out into two of that suit; an important point in this connection is that even 2♣ is a weakness take-out here: there is no Stayman convention once the 1NT has been doubled. And if you have a weak balanced hand with nowhere to go, you just have to pass and wish your partner the very best of luck. Unless you and your regular partner have devised some complicated escape machinery, I would strongly advise against trying to wriggle out of trouble when you have only four-card suits, for you might well make matters even worse by forcing the bidding to the two level. In fact, almost the only situation in which you might be able to effect a Houdini-type escape act is something like the following:

♠ 10 7 6 4
♡ 9 8 3 2
◇ J 7 5 4
♣ 8

If you hold this depressing hand and partner's opening bid of 1NT is doubled, you know that he is in for a pretty rough time. If you are feeling venturesome, therefore, you might try the effect of bidding 2♣! This will almost certainly be doubled, and you can now redouble to invite partner to choose between the other three suits. This kind of redouble can scarcely be natural in this sort of sequence and this is a good example of the so-called SOS Redouble. If it succeeds in locating a 4–4 fit in spades, hearts or diamonds, it should save your side a few hundred points.

If the opponents overcall 1NT with two of a suit, you can afford to be quick on the trigger with a penalty double if you have a reasonable holding in trumps and if you know that your side has the balance of the points. Think twice before you double with a poor holding in their suit, however; what I call a purely 'Point Count Double' can be extremely expensive.

♠ A 7 2
♡ 9 3
◇ Q 10 5 3
♣ 10 8 6 4

If the bidding starts with 1NT by partner and 2♡ on your right, you know that your side has a majority of at least 22 to 18 in high-card points. However, it would be quite wrong to double; your right-hand opponent knew that he was missing a lot of points when he decided to enter the auction, and he is marked with a good heart suit; what is more, your poor holding in hearts makes it almost certain that the trumps are breaking kindly and that any missing honours in hearts will be favourably placed for the opponents. If the enemy were to come in with 2◇ instead of 2♡, of course, you would have an ideal penalty double on the above hand: you now know that the declarer is going to run into a bad trump break and that the hand is going to contain one or two nasty surprises for him.

An extremely important point to bear in mind when the opponents overcall an opening bid of 1NT is that any non-jump response in a new suit by the opener's partner is not forcing—even if it is made at the three level.

♠ 7 4
♡ K 7 2
◇ 10 9
♣ Q 10 8 7 4 3

If the auction starts 1NT–2♠, it is quite safe to compete with 3♣; partner should not regard this as a strong bid, and he will normally pass. In fact, he will only bid on if the knowledge that you have a six-card club suit and the values to compete makes his hand much stronger; if, for example, he has A–K–x in clubs and a good holding in spades, he might be in a position to have a shot at 3NT.

Another useful manoeuvre available to the responder is to bid the suit in which the opponents have overcalled.

♠ K J 7 5
♡ 10 4
◇ 7 5 3
♣ A Q 8 2

Opposite an opening bid of 1NT, this hand clearly contains the values for game. Normally, you would use the Stayman 2♣ convention to see if there is a 4–4 spade fit between the two hands, prepared to settle in 3NT if the response to 2♣ is 2◇ or 2♡. However, let us suppose that your right-hand opponent comes in with 2♡ over 1NT. This hand is not well-suited for a penalty double, particularly if your side is vulnerable and stands to score more by bidding and making game, and yet you can no longer employ Stayman to search for a spade fit. The answer is to bid an immediate 3♡: this is forcing to game, and it gives partner the choice of showing a four-card spade suit or rebidding 3NT if he has a good holding in hearts.

5

Slam Bidding

Slam bidding is really too big a topic to condense into a fairly short chapter of a fairly short book. It is, in fact, a subject to which experts have, over the years, devoted a great deal of time and a great many books and articles, and yet the accuracy of slam bidding in international matches and other important events all too often leaves much to be desired. All I can do is to run through a number of important points, starting with a look at the kinds of auction which often lead to the investigation of a slam contract.

A number of sequences which lead up to an eventual slam, or at least to a slam try, stem from a strength-showing opening bid. Probably the most straightforward of these openings, because it defines the hand within fairly narrow limits, is 2NT; this shows a balanced hand with 20–22 points, and the responder should always be aware of the possibility of a slam if he has 10 points or more. His first task should normally be to search for an eight-card trump fit for, while the partnership will generally need a total of 33 or 34 points to make 6NT, this figure can be reduced by 3 or 4 points if a suit fit can be found. For example:

West	East
♠ A J 8 4	♠ K Q 9 5 2
♡ K 7	♡ A 10 4
◇ A K 7 2	◇ 9 5
♣ K Q J	♣ 8 7 6

West opens 2NT and East makes the forcing response of 3♠, showing a five-card spade suit and the values for game. With such an excellent fit for his partner's suit and such good controls, West should not simply make a sleepy raise to 4♠, which might end the auction. His correct bid is 4◇; this is called an advance cue bid, agreeing spades, showing the ace of diamonds, and, because it is normal to make the cheapest possible cue bid first, denying the ace of clubs. Over 4♦, East can show that he also has something to spare by cue-bidding his ace of hearts, and nothing should now keep West out of the excellent 6♠ contract. Always look out for the opportunity to make an advance cue bid of this kind: it is often the only safe way of suggesting the possibility of a slam without getting the bidding too high. The 4♦ bid in this example can never cost: if East has a minimum hand on which he has just scraped together a bid of 3♠, he can sign off in 4♠ over 4♦ and no damage will have been done.

It is also possible to reach a suit slam after an opening bid of 2NT by way of a conventional response of 3♣. I personally like to play a simple Stayman-like 3♣ convention over 2NT, just asking the opener to show a four-card major suit if he has one. Most experts, however, prefer to play what is known as the Baron Convention, whereby 3♣ asks the opener to bid his four-card suits in ascending order, so that any 4-4 fit will be found.

West	East
♠ A Q 10 4	♠ K J 7 3
♡ K 7	♡ A 6 3
◇ A K 9 2	◇ 8 5
♣ A J 5	♣ Q 10 9 6

In response to his partner's opening bid of 2NT, East bids 3♣ in an effort to find a 4-4 suit fit. Playing Baron, West shows his diamond suit, and the 4-4 spade fit comes to light when East rebids 3♠ over 3◇. Once again West should not simply make a lazy raise to 4♠: with his excellent trump support and good controls, he cue bids 4♣ to agree spades and to suggest to this partner that a slam is a distinct possibility. East also has something to spare, and he announces this by bidding 4♡ to show the ace of hearts; the excellent spade slam should now be reached with no further difficulty.

The strongest opening bid of all is, of course, 2♣. It is used on all balanced hands containing 23 or more points and on all other hands of game-going strength; there is, in fact, only one sequence (2♣–2◇–2NT) after which the auction can die below the game level. I personally like to play the CAB system of responses to 2♣, whereby the responder's first duty is to show his ace holding: 2♡, 2♠, 3♣ or 3◇ shows the ace of the bid suit; 3NT shows two aces; 2◇ shows no ace and 0–7 points; and 2NT shows no ace and at least 8 points.

Ace-showing responses often make it extremely simple to reach the correct slam contract.

West	East
♠ K 9 5	♠ A 8 4
♡ None	♡ J 9 3
◇ A K J 10	◇ Q 9 8 6 4 2
♣ A K 10 9 8 3	♣ 7

West opens 2♣ and East makes the helpful response of 2♠, showing that he holds the ace of spades and no other ace. West now shows his club suit and is once again pleasantly surprised to hear his partner bid 3◇. In an effort to find out more about the distribution of East's hand, West makes the waiting bid of 4♣; when East rebids 4◇, showing that he has at the most two clubs and almost certainly a singleton or a void, West can be certain that 7◇ must be an excellent contract, even if the combined values of the two hands are quite minimum; he therefore bids the grand slam without further ado.

Playing normal Acol, the responses to 2♣ are slightly different, in that the responder attempts to show his general values on the first round instead of identifying his precise ace holding. In the original Acol system, the requirements for a positive response to 2♣ were extremely rigid and took the form of an elaborate list of honour-trick qualifications which the responder very rarely held in practice. The modern tendency is to make the bidding after 2♣ more fluid and flexible by reducing the standards for a positive response to a more reasonable level. For a positive response at the two level, it is now generally agreed that a goodish five-card suit with a little outside is enough, and this in itself often makes it easier to reach a good slam contract.

West	East
♠ A K 9 4	♠ 7 2
♡ A Q 7	♡ K J 10 4 2
◇ Q J 8 3	◇ K 6
♣ A K	♣ J 10 8 5

In response to his partner's opening bid of 2♣, East has enough by present-day standards for a positive response of 2♡. West's best rebid is probably a waiting bid of 2NT, and East shows his second suit by bidding 3♣. West now bids 3♡ and East, who has done more than enough already, signs off in 4♡. West, however, has a very suitable hand opposite his partner's bidding, and he should make a slam try by cue-bidding 4♠; East, who has limited his hand by bidding 4♡ on the previous round, should co-operate by showing his diamond feature, and this makes it easy for West to bid 6♡—an excellent contract.

A positive response at the three level over 2♣ should still show a slightly better hand, for it takes up so much more bidding space. Generally speaking, a goodish suit and one and a half tricks are the minimum requirements for a response at the three level.

The third form of strong opening bid available to the opener is an Acol Two. 2◇, 2♡ or 2♠ shows an extremely strong hand with at least eight playing tricks, and is forcing for one round. The suit will normally contain at least six cards, but it is sometimes desirable to open with an Acol Two bid on a powerful hand with a 5–5 distribution.

West	East
♠ A K Q 5 2	♠ 6 3
♡ A 8	♡ 7 5 4 2
◇ A Q J 9 5	◇ K 10 6 4
♣ 7	♣ A 9 3

The West hand clearly qualifies for an opening bid of 2♠, even though it is only based on a five-card suit. East makes the negative response of 2NT for the time being, but his hand becomes really strong when West shows his second suit by rebidding 3◇. East's best bid at this stage is probably 4♣, which can logically only be a cue bid agreeing diamonds: it is inconceivable that East would wish to introduce a club suit of his own at this point, now that his partner has shown a powerful two-suited hand. Even if West is temporarily confused by the 4♣ bid, everything will become clear when it is followed by diamond support from East, and the excellent small slam in diamonds should be reached with little difficulty.

The responses to an Acol Two bid are similar to those to a 2♣ opening, in that to introduce a new suit shows a good suit with either one honour trick at the two level or one and a half honour tricks at the three level. In addition, the responder can raise the opener's suit immediately if he has some kind of trump support and fair values; a raise to the three level promises an ace or a void suit somewhere in the hand, and a jump denies holding a first-round control.

West	East
♠ A K J 10 7 4	♠ Q 9 6 5
♡ K 2	♡ A 8 3
◇ A K Q	◇ J 9 7 5 3
♣ J 8	♣ 7

Opposite an opening 2♠ bid by his partner, East shows that he has trump support and an ace by raising to 3♠. West now cue bids 4◇, and East shows his ace by bidding 4♡ in reply. At this point, West is in a certain amount of difficulty for, while he is still interested in a slam, he is understandably very worried about those two losing clubs. He can actually convey his anxiety to his partner by jumping to 5♠ over 4♡. A jump to five of this kind is often extremely useful when the partnership is in the hunt for a slam; it shows precisely two losers in the unbid suit and asks partner to bid six if he has second-round control of the suit in question, to cue bid if he has first-round control, or to pass if he also has at least two losers in the critical suit.

The immediate jump to four after the opener's strong two bid is often a great help to bidding a slam—and even more often a great help to not bidding one!

West	East
♠ A K J 10 7 4	♠ Q 9 8 5 2
♡ K Q	♡ J 9
◇ A K J	◇ 10 8 7 4
♣ J 5	♣ K Q

As you will see, even a contract of 5♠ is in jeopardy on this badly-fitting pair of hands, but there should be little danger of East–West getting too high. West opens 2♠ and, when East jumps to 4♠, showing good trump support and denying any first-round control, West will know that there must be at least two top losers on the hand and will not be tempted to move forward.

So much for slam bidding when it is the opener who has a powerful hand. Many possible slam contracts come to light when the opener starts with a simple one bid and it is the responder who has a very strong holding. Generally speaking, the responder should make what is often called a 'forcing take-out', that is, a jump response in a new suit, if he has 16 points or more. Such a jump is forcing to game, and it may be the vital first move in reaching a slam if the opener also has something in reserve.

As we have already seen in Chapter 2, it is also possible to make a jump response on fewer than 16 points, principally when you have an excellent fit for partner's suit or when you have a very good, self-supporting suit of your own.

Talking about forcing on good suits brings me to a convention which is often overlooked but which can sometimes be an invaluable aid to slam bidding. In Chapter 2, we considered a hand containing 13 points and ♡AKQ10 9 7 on which it is undoubtedly correct to jump to 2♡ after an opening bid of 1♣ or 1◇ by your partner. Now let us suppose that we make that hand just slightly stronger:

♠ 10 8
♡ A K Q J 10 9
◇ 5 3
♣ A 7 4

Once again it is best to force with 2♡ if partner opens 1♣ or 1♢, but now if partner makes a minimum rebid like 2♠, 2NT or 3♣, the correct rebid is a second jump, this time to 4♡. A jump of this kind, that is, a jump in a situation which is already forcing to game, shows a solid suit which will make a playable trump suit even opposite a void; it is often the key bid in a successful slam sequence.

West	East
♠ A K Q J 10 8	♠ 6
♡ K 7 3	♡ A J 8
♢ 8 6	♢ A 7 5 4
♣ 5 2	♣ A K Q 10 4

If West opens 1♠ and East makes the forcing-to-game response of 3♣, West's best rebid is a jump to 4♠, showing a solid spade suit. When East now asks for aces and kings and finds that there is one king in the red suits, he will be able to count twelve absolutely certain tricks and should realize that 7♠ must be an excellent proposition.

No discussion of slam bidding would be complete without mentioning what is probably the most popular convention of all: the Blackwood 4NT bid. Unfortunately, it is probably true to say that this convention is only so popular because it is employed a great deal more often than it should be. My own view is that Blackwood should usually only be used to keep you out of a bad slam, and not to get you into a good one.

♠ 10 4
♡ K J 9 7 2
♢ A 5
♣ A 8 6 3

Suppose that partner opens 1♢ opposite this hand and then raises your 1♡ response to 3♡. Although you should clearly be thinking about 6♡ at this point, this is just the sort of hand on which you should *not* use Blackwood. For one thing, it is possible to imagine a hand on which partner holds both the missing aces and on which there is nevertheless very little chance of making 6♡; and, more important, there are many hands on which one of the aces is missing and yet which will make 6♡ a simple contract.

♠ 9
♡ A Q 10 4
♢ K Q J 8 2
♣ K 9 5

This hand, for example, will make 6♡ fairly comfortably opposite the hand given earlier, but are you going to bid the slam if you bid 4NT and find that one of the aces is missing? The answer clearly is that you are not, for there could well be two losing spades in each hand, and this means that Blackwood is not the best answer. It is much more efficient to show your slam interest by cue-bidding 4♣ over 3♡ instead of crudely wheeling out Blackwood; by subsequently showing your concern about the spade suit, you should be able to investigate slam possibilities more clearly and more accurately.

You may have noticed that, in almost all the slam sequences which I have suggested so far in this chapter, I have recommended the use of cue bids at some stage of the auction. I personally think that cue bids are more useful in good slam bidding than all the various 4♣ and 4NT ace-asking conventions rolled into one, and I strongly recommend that you should practise cue-bidding as much as possible, only using Blackwood on hands on which you are certain that to find out how many aces your partner has will solve all your problems and tell you how high the final contract should be. Such hands do, of course, exist.

♠ K
♡ K Q 10 7 5
♢ K Q J 6 3
♣ K 4

Suppose that you open 1♡ on this hand and that the auction proceeds 1♡–1♠–2♢–4♡. Your partner has shown game-going values with four-card heart support and a reasonable spade suit, and it is clear that all you need to find out at this point is how many aces there are opposite. Bid 4NT, Black-wood. If partner bids 5♡, showing two aces, that should prove to be a perfectly safe contract; and if the response is 5♠, showing three aces, you can bid what must be an excellent small slam in hearts.

6

Defensive Bidding

I have often thought how much easier the bidding would be if
we could play bridge against two silent, unimaginative opponents who were only allowed to bid if it was perfectly clear to
everybody that the hand really belonged to them. In real life, of
course, we often find the opponents striving to get into the act
on very limited values; their only objective in these cases is to be
awkward, pushing us up a little higher than we really want to go
and making it difficult for us to exchange information in a calm,
unhurried bidding sequence. That is their job, and I mentioned
in Chapter 2 the ways in which the responder should attempt to
deal with opposing overcalls and take-out doubles after his
partner has opened the bidding. On as many as half the hands
you play at the table, of course, the opponents will go one stage
further and actually open the bidding, and I must now go on to
consider the various ways in which you can enter the auction
after an opening bid by the enemy. This is a very important
aspect of the game which is called in bridge language 'defensive
bidding'.

If your opponent has opened the bidding with one of a suit,
the usual way of entering the auction is by way of a simple
overcall in another suit; in fact, it is probably true to say that the
simple suit overcall is used *too* much, for, as I hope to show a
little later on, it is often far safer to enter the auction by making a
take-out double. When you are contemplating a suit overcall,
don't worry too much about how many points you hold; it is far
more important to consider the playing strength of your hand
and the quality of your suit, for these are the factors which will
determine your fate if the worst happens and your overcall is
doubled for penalties.

♠ A 7
♡ J 7 4 3 2
♢ Q 9 5
♣ K 10 6
(Hand A)

♠ A 7
♡ K Q J 9 5
♢ 9 7 5
♣ 10 8 3
(Hand B)

These two hands both contain a five-card heart suit and 10 high-card points, but only Hand B warrants an overcall of 1♡ if your right-hand opponent opens the bidding in one of the minors. The poor quality of the trump suit in Hand A may lead to a severe penalty if you are doubled in 1♡; furthermore, the fact that so many heart honours are missing makes it much more likely that the opponents will be in a position to make a penalty double. On Hand B, however, you are almost certain to come to five tricks even if your partner's hand is completely worthless, and there is very little danger in making a simple overcall of 1♡. What is more, there is much more point in overcalling with Hand B, for you would certainly welcome a heart lead if the opponents eventually play the contract and your partner is on lead.

In theory, a suit overcall should guarantee at least a five-card suit; furthermore, if the overcall has to be made at the two level, it should be based on a six-card or very strong five-card suit. In practice, of course. it is often good tactics to get into the bidding on hands which do not quite match up to these rigid requirements, and there are two important factors which you should bear in mind when contemplating whether or not to make a flimsy overcall. The first is the vulnerability; if the game score is in your favour, you may well be able to make life very awkward for your vulnerable opponents, and it may well be possible for you to find a worthwhile sacrifice bid if they reach game. The second point is a less obvious one and concerns the bidding space taken up by your overcall: it is clearly far more damaging to the opponents if you can bid 1♠ over their 1♣ than if your overcall is a mere 1♢, for the spade overcall will deprive them of a complete round of bidding in which they could usefully have exchanged information. Always look out for the opportunity of making a space-consuming overcall like 1♣–1♠, 1♢–2♣,

1♡–2◇ or 1♠–2♡, for these bids are liable to be much more effective than other overcalls.

Bearing these two points in mind, there is often a lot to be said for making a risky overcall on a four-card suit if the conditions are right.

♠ A K J 10
♡ 10 8
◇ Q 7 6 3
♣ 9 6 4

Not vulnerable, I would probably venture an overcall of 1♠ over a 1♣ opening on my right; while this bid is slightly risky in that my partner will expect me to have a longer spade suit, the pre-emptive effect of the spade overcall makes it a worthwhile gamble. Furthermore, the overcall indicates a good opening lead to partner if my left-hand opponent eventually plays the hand, and it may make it extremely difficult for them to settle in a no trump contract.

As I mentioned earlier, it is difficult to count points in relation to an overcall. However, for those of you who like to be able to use points as a rough guide in as many situations as possible, I would suggest that a simple suit overcall should not be made on a hand containing more than 12 high-card points. This means, of course, that partner needs a rather stronger hand to respond to an overcall than to respond to an opening bid, and, unless his hand is particularly suitable, he should not respond in a non-competitive situation with less than 9 points.

♠ J 4
♡ J 8 5 2
◇ K 7 3
♣ A Q 10 4

If your left-hand opponent opens 1♣ and your partner overcalls with 1♠, bid 1NT on this hand. All no trump bids are constructive in response to an overcall, and I would recommend that you should use a minimum response in no trumps to show 10–12 points with a good holding in the opponents' suit; with 13–15 points, a jump response in no trumps is in order.

One final thought on responding to overcalls: since the overcaller has promised at least five cards in his suit, partner can feel free to raise the overcall with as little as three small cards or a doubleton honour in support.

♠ A J 6 5
♡ Q 7
◇ K 10 8 3
♣ 9 6 5

If partner bids 1♡ over the opening bid of 1♣ and the next player competes with 2♣, you should have no hesitation in raising to 2♡. Although you would prefer to have better trump support than Q–x, partner should have a good heart suit for his overcall and 2♡ should prove to be a perfectly playable contract.

If you have a one-suited hand which is too strong for a simple overcall, the correct action will probably be a jump overcall; this shows a six-card or extremely strong five-card suit and six or seven playing tricks. A jump overcall is not forcing, but it is a highly descriptive bid and partner should be in a good position to judge whether to pass, support the overcall or convert to a no trump contract.

♠ A K J 10 7 4
♡ 8 4
◇ A J 8
♣ 7 6

Over an opening bid of 1♣, 1◇ or 1♡ on your right, this hand is just about worth a jump overcall of 2♠. Such an overcall may be made on a slightly weaker hand than this; if your hand is much stronger and still one-suited, it will have to be shown by an immediate jump to 4♠ or by a take-out double followed by a jump in spades.

A jump overcall shows a strong hand with a long suit equal to opening bid of one in that suit. If you have similar strength and a balanced hand, the correct overcall will probably be 1NT, which shows 16–18 points and a good holding in the opponents' suit; ideally, this holding should be a double stop, and you should at least have the possibility of taking two tricks in the suit.

♠ A Q 10
♡ 10 8
◇ A K 9 7 4
♣ K J 3

You have an obvious double of an opening bid of 1♡ on this hand; over 1♣ or 1♠ on your right, however, by far the best action is to overcall 1NT. Don't worry too much about the weak holding in hearts: an overcall of 1NT describes this hand accurately in one bid, and it doesn't sound as if the heart suit is going to be too much of a threat—after all, if one of the opponents does have considerable length in the suit, it will almost certainly be the hand on your left, who will have very few entries.

If you have an even stronger hand (that is, 19 or more points) with a guard in the opponents' suit, the correct action is to make a take-out double first and to rebid in no trumps on the next round. For example:

♠ J 4
♡ K Q 8
◇ A Q 9
♣ A K 10 7 3

If your right-hand opponent opens 1◇ or 1♡, you should make a take-out double on this hand, planning to rebid 1NT over the likely response of 1♠. This will show a balanced hand with 19–20 points.

This brings me to what is often the safest way of entering the auction after an opening bid by the opponents: the take-out double. This is the most popular conventional bid in bridge, for an immediate double of one of a suit is universally used as a request for partner to bid his longest suit. Ideally, the double should show a hand with shortage in the opponents' suit and support for any suit which partner cares to name. In practice, of course, the take-out double is used on a variety of other hands, and I always emphasize to my partners that they must not expect too much from my doubles; I feel quite strongly that it is important to enter the auction as soon as possible if I have the values and, broadly speaking, I am inclined to double if I have an opening bid and no strong suit of my own.

♠ A 10 7 4
♡ Q J 8 2
◇ K 7
♣ A 9 3

Over an opening bid of 1◇, this hand constitutes a classical take-out double, for it has adequate support for all three unbid suits. But now let us suppose that your right-hand opponent opens 1♣. In this case, some of the more rigid textbooks might recommend a pass, but I would certainly not agree with such a pessimistic view: with 14 points and good support for both major suits, a take-out double still stands to gain far more than it stands to lose and, even though there is a slight risk that partner might end up doubled in a diamond contract, it would be equally risky to pass on this hand and find yourself completely shut out of the auction.

There are other situations in which it is correct to make a take-out double even if you only have support for *two* of the unbid suits. For example:

♠ A Q 7 4
♡ 7 5
◇ A K J 8 3
♣ 10 4

Over an opening bid of 1♡, a take-out double is preferable to a simple overcall of 2◇. It is important to find a spade fit if there is one and, when you come to think of it, a double is most unlikely to come to any harm: if partner is forced to bid clubs over the double, you can still convert to diamonds without raising the level of the bidding.

Similarly, there are certain hands on which you have to make a take-out double for the simple reason that you are too strong for any other bid.

♠ A Q 8 5 4
♡ 7 3
◇ A 5
♣ A K J 3

Over a 1♡ opening bid on your right, this hand is much too strong for a simple overcall of 1♠, but the spade suit is not really good enough to warrant an immediate jump to 2♠. You will therefore have to double and, if partner makes the likely response of 2◇, you can show the nature of your hand by converting to 2♠. This is obviously a strength-showing sequence, and it might enable partner to make a further bid if he has a suitable hand.

The responses to a take-out double are fairly straight-forward. There is just one important point which I must emphasize: remember that you will be forced to respond to a double even if you have a four-card suit and no points at all; if you have something worthwhile to report, therefore, you must tell partner the good news by making a jump response in your best suit.

♠ A J 7 4 2
♡ 7 5 2
◇ K 8 3
♣ 10 4

If partner doubles an opening bid of 1♣, 1◇ or 1♡, you should show your values by jumping to 2♠. A jump response of this kind is not forcing; partner will pass if he has a minimum hand for his original double but, if he has something to spare, your encouraging response might enable him to go on to game.

The fact that a jump response is not forcing means, of course, that you must make a correspondingly stronger response if your hand is even better than the last one. For example, let us add another ace.

♠ A J 7 4 2
♡ 7 5 2
◇ K 8 3
♣ A 4

You now have enough for game opposite partner's take-out double, and there is no reason not to jump to 4♠ direct. What you must *not* do is to make a simple jump to 2♠, for partner might pass this and miss a comfortable game. If you are in any doubt as to how high to go in this kind of situation, I would like to suggest that you apply the following simple rule. Imagine that partner has opened one of the suit you are planning to bid: if you would raise him to game, bid game now; if you would make a jump raise in his suit, make a jump response to the double.

There are, of course, hands on which the responder cannot be completely certain of the best final resting place, even though his partner has made a take-out double.

> ♠ K Q 7 2
> ♡ A J 8 3
> ◇ K 10 4
> ♣ 9 6

If your partner doubles the opening bid of 1♣ or 1◇, your best action is to bid two of the opponents' suit; you can then jump to game in whichever major suit partner bids.

It is also possible to bid the opponents' suit on slightly weaker hands.

> ♠ K Q 7 2
> ♡ A J 8 3
> ◇ 7 4
> ♣ 10 8 2

If your partner doubles the opening bid of 1◇, the best response is again an immediate cue bid of 2◇, planning to raise 2♡ or 2♠ to three. To bid the opponents' suit opposite a take-out double is not completely forcing to game, and a raise to 3♡ or 3♠ in this kind of sequence is merely an invitational limit raise, showing the sort of hand on which you would have raised an opening bid of 1♡ or 1♠ to the same level.

Another very important point to bear in mind when you are contemplating your response to a take-out double is that a no trump response should always show positive values.

♠ 7 2
♡ 10 8 4
◇ Q J 10 7
♣ 10 9 6 3

If partner doubles an opening bid of 1◇, you must reject the temptation to bid 1NT, for that would be a positive response promising 6–9 points. You must make the natural response of 2♣ or, if you feel like taking a slight risk in an effort to keep the bidding low, you might experiment with a response of 1♡.

1NT is often the correct response even when you have considerable length in the opponents' suit.

♠ J 10 5
♡ 9 6
◇ A Q 7 4 2
♣ Q 3 2

If partner doubles the opening bid of 1◇, bid 1NT. Average players often make the mistake of passing on this kind of hand, thereby converting the double into a penalty double, but it is very rarely wise to pass the double unless you have a really solid holding in the trump suit. You will always find a low level contract difficult to defend when the long trump suit is situated *over* you, and the best hope for the defence is that they will be able to draw the declarer's trumps, leaving the original doubler free to take tricks with his high cards in the side suits; for this reason, it is important to have a really solid holding in the trump suit before you consider passing a take-out double at the one level.

So much for defensive bidding after the opponents have opened the bidding with *one* of a suit. Far more difficult situations arise if the opening is a pre-emptive three bid, suggesting a seven-card or longer suit and a weak hand. Our problem now is that we only have one or two rounds of bidding left in which to decide how high we should go and in which denomination we should play, and this is often an extremely difficult task. The one certain point is that you must have an agreed method of announcing a strongish hand and requesting partner to bid his best suit at the appropriate level, and several conventions have been devised over the years to deal with opposing pre-empts. I have experimented with most of them. Fishbein, Lower Minor, Herbert, 3NT for a take-out, Optional Double, X–4–X etc. all have certain advantages, but none of them is 100% efficient; in fact, none of them is much more than 50% efficient, and that is why the pre-emptive three has survived as an effective, and at times devastating, weapon for so many years.

My own view, based on many years' experience, is that the best counter to an opening pre-empt is an informatory double. This has the merit of complete simplicity, and has the advantage of keeping the bidding as low as you possibly can, as well as allowing you to overcall in any of the three suits in a completely natural sense. Remember, however, that you must have quite a strong hand to enter the auction with an informatory double immediately over an opening three bid, particularly if your partner is likely to have to respond at the four level and particularly if he has already passed. There is no reason to assume that your partner has more than his fair share of the outstanding high-card strength. Furthermore, to make matters worse, if it turns out to be your left-hand opponent who has the strong hand, the opening three bid has made it unlikely that your long suits will be breaking evenly for you. If the pre-empt is followed by two passes, of course, it is safer to double on a slightly weaker hand. Furthermore, a fourth-in-hand double will more often be passed for penalties by the doubler's partner, for he is more likely to have a worthwhile trump holding when he is situated *over* the declarer rather than on his right.

A final point about dealing with pre-empts. Whatever methods you and your partner agree to employ in defence, there is one thing on which I am absolutely convinced: you *must* reserve an overcall of 3NT as a natural bid in any position.

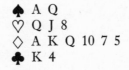

$$\spadesuit \text{ A Q}$$
$$\heartsuit \text{ Q J 8}$$
$$\diamondsuit \text{ A K Q 10 7 5}$$
$$\clubsuit \text{ K 4}$$

Over an opening bid of 3♡ or 3♠, or even 3♣, you will find yourself in terrible difficulties if your methods do not permit you to bid a direct 3NT 'to play'. Pre-empts are bound to make life difficult for us on certain hands; we simply have to cope as best we can, and we shall not do too badly if we are prepared to take our medicine on some hands and if we are able to deal satisfactorily with situations like the one above.

7

The Play of a
No Trump Contract

It has been said that more contracts are won or lost at the first trick than at any other stage of the hand, and I can't help thinking that this is certainly true. In the first place, trick one is the time when you should be making your general plan of campaign for the hand, counting your obvious tricks and working out where any additional tricks which you require are to come from; secondly, the suit led to the first trick will more often than not be the suit which the opponents will be hoping first to establish and later to cash against you, and you will have to consider whether there is any way in which you can nullify the effect of their long suit; and finally, your choice of the actual cards to play to the first trick may in itself determine the eventual fate of the contract. In this chapter, I shall go through each of these points in a little more detail and try to show you the sort of way in which the declarer should be thinking in the early stages of a no trump contract.

Generally speaking, it should be easier to formulate your plan of campaign in a no trump contract than in a suit contract, for the absence of a trump suit means that there are fewer lines of play available to the declarer and the most promising source of the extra tricks which you have to develop will normally be fairly obvious. Against that, no trump contracts often have to be handled with considerable care and attention, for the simple reason that you haven't got the protection which is offered by a long trump suit. I strongly recommend that you should always stop to think about the hand as a whole before playing a card to the first trick. Don't feel guilty about delaying the proceedings while you think things over: there is no reward on the score-sheet for playing quickly, and the fate of your contract may well depend on a little clear thinking while you are making your plan.

The first important point to remember is not to be greedy: always choose the line of play which will give you the *best* chance of making the contract rather than the one which *might* give you the most tricks.

	West		East
			(Dummy)
♠	A Q 5	♠	K 7 3
♡	7 2	♡	A K J 8 4
◇	8 6 4 3	◇	A K 2
♣	J 9 8 3	♣	K 10

Suppose that you are the declarer in 3NT on this deal and that North leads the jack of spades. When you count your top tricks, you will find seven: three spades, two hearts and two diamonds. It is tempting to look to dummy's excellent heart suit for the extra tricks; in fact, if it is your lucky day and you find North with queen to three hearts, you will be in the running for eleven or even twelve tricks in the end game. To play on hearts is not, however, the best way of ensuring nine tricks on this hand, for life will become very awkward if you find that most of the missing hearts are in the South hand and he switches his attack to diamonds. There is, in fact, a line of play which absolutely guarantees that you will make your contract: win the spade lead in dummy and play the king of clubs. By preserving the entries to your hand and driving out the ace and queen of clubs as soon as you can, you can be 100% sure of developing two tricks in the suit, and therefore 100% sure of making your game contract.

Sometimes it will not be possible to find a line of play which will absolutely guarantee success. In these situations, it is important to look for the line which will give you the *best* chance of making the contract.

	West		East
			(Dummy)
♠	K 7 2	♠	A 8 4
♡	K 4	♡	A 7
◇	A 10 6	◇	K J 9 7 3
♣	8 7 6 5 4	♣	K Q J

North leads the queen of hearts against your contract of 3 NT. You have six top tricks and, since the opponents are threatening to establish their heart suit and you can only afford to lose the lead once more, it is clearly vital for you to find the best way of developing the three additional tricks which you require. The choice lies between taking the diamond finesse, which, to all intents and purposes, will succeed whenever North has the queen of diamonds, and knocking out the ace of clubs, which will produce nine tricks whenever the adverse clubs break 3–2. Since the clubs will break favourably more than two-thirds of the time and the queen of diamonds will be in the North hand only half the time, the best line of play is clearly to lead a club at the second trick. And there is more to it than that. If you try the clubs first and find that they are divided 4–1, you can still fall back on the diamond finesse for the contract. However, the reverse is not true. If you take the diamond finesse first and it loses, you will not be able to fall back on the club suit without losing too many tricks in hearts.

One of the important points to think about when you are planning your play of the hand is the entry situation. If you look back to the first hand which I discussed earlier, you will remember how the correct play was to win the first spade lead in dummy, in order to preserve the entries in your hand to establish and enjoy the club tricks. Sometimes your entry problems will be even more acute than this, and you may find that the only hope lies in ducking a round or two of the critical suit.

West	East
	(Dummy)
♠ A Q 6 2	♠ 10 7 4
♡ A Q 5	♡ K
◇ A K 4	◇ 9 7 5 3
♣ 8 6 5	♣ A 10 7 4 2

Once again you are the declarer in 3 NT, this time against the lead of the jack of hearts. The first thing to do, as always, is to count your tricks, and you will find that you have seven tricks readily available. The best chance of two more is clearly to play clubs in such a manner that, if the suit breaks 3–2, you can make the two long clubs in dummy. Unfortunately, however, the opening lead has prematurely removed dummy's only side entry, and the only way of reaching the long clubs is now via the ace of clubs itself. This means that you will have to establish the clubs by ducking two rounds of the suit; then, if the suit breaks reasonably, you will be able to enter dummy with the ace of clubs on the third round in order to cash the two established winners.

A ducking play of this kind may be correct even if it is quite likely that you can make the contract by other means.

West	East
	(Dummy)
♠ A K 4	♠ 9 7 3
♡ A Q 7	♡ 8 6
◇ 6 5	◇ A K Q 9 8 2
♣ Q 10 9 4 2	♣ 7 6

Once again North leads the jack of hearts against your contract of 3 NT. This time you have seven top tricks and it is clear that you can look to dummy's powerful diamond suit to provide the two additional tricks which you require. In fact, of course, if the adverse diamonds are divided 3–2, as is likely, you can make all six diamond tricks and ten tricks in all, but here we come back to the point which I made earlier about not being greedy. You don't need to make all the diamonds for the contract; five diamond tricks will do nicely, and you should therefore duck the first round of the suit just in case. This will ensure that you make five tricks in diamonds even if the suit is breaking 4–1; after all, the possible loss of an overtrick is a small price to pay to ensure that you will make your game contract even if there is a bad distribution.

Ducking can sometimes be the only way of sorting things out when your comings and goings are really tangled.

West

♠ A 10 3
♡ A 9 5
♢ 9 5 4 2
♣ A K 2

East
(Dummy)

♠ 8 6 4 2
♡ K
♢ A K 7
♣ 9 7 5 4 3

North leads the king of spades against your contract of 3NT. You can count seven tricks in top cards, and the best chance of the two extra tricks which you need lies in finding the opponents' clubs divided 3–2 and in establishing two long clubs in dummy. You duck the first spade and, when South follows twice, you win the second round with the ace. Assuming the clubs are kind, the only problem now is one of entries. If you play the ace, king and a third club in order to establish the suit, you will subsequently have no way of getting back to your hand to enjoy the ace of hearts; and if you cash the top hearts before losing the inevitable club trick, the defenders will be able to take too many heart tricks when they gain the lead. The solution to the problem is that you should immediately duck a club after winning the ace of spades: the top clubs will now provide an entry for the ace of hearts, and dummy's top diamonds will allow you to get there to cash the long club tricks.

I have so far only considered the declarer's early play in a no trump contract from the point of view of the tricks which he is planning to establish and make for himself. He also has to worry about the tricks which the opponents are threatening to develop and, since the defenders have the benefit of the opening lead, he will often find that they have a head start in the race for tricks. One of the principal ways in which the declarer can forestall his opponents is the hold-up play, and here again the play to the first trick will often be crucial.

West

♠ A 8 4
♡ K 9 5
♢ J 10 2
♣ A 9 6 5

East
(Dummy)

♠ 10 6
♡ A J 3
♢ K Q 9 6 4
♣ K 10 2

Imagine that you are West, the declarer in 3NT, and that North leads the 3 of spades to his partner's queen. You clearly plan to make nine tricks by way of one spade, two hearts, four diamonds and two clubs and, if the adverse spades are divided 4–4, nothing can stop you from making your contract in this way. If the spades are not breaking evenly, however, the position of the ace of diamonds will be all-important, and you should hold up the ace of spades until the third round in case South has the ace of diamonds and only three spades. South will then not have a spade left when he eventually gains the lead, and North will no longer be able to cash his two established tricks.

The question of whether or not to hold up usually only arises when the declarer has the ace of the suit led, but it can also pay to withhold other definite tricks until a later round.

West	East (Dummy)
♠ K 9 3	♠ A 10 4
♡ K J 6	♡ 8 3 2
◇ Q J 10 4	◇ A 9 7 5
♣ A 8 5	♣ K Q 10

You are the declarer in 3NT, and North leads the 5 of hearts to his partner's queen. If the adverse hearts are divided 4–3, nothing will defeat the contract; the worrying situation is where North has led from a five-card heart suit and his partner has the king of diamonds, for now, if you win the first trick with the king of hearts, South will return his second heart when he gains the lead and you will be doomed to defeat. The answer is to treat your king-jack of hearts as though they were the ace and to duck the queen of hearts at the first trick; South can return his second heart immediately, but, if the suit is divided 5–2, he will then not have another heart to play if he gets in with the king of diamonds. Notice that the situation would be completely different if the diamond holdings of East and West were reversed; it would now be perfectly safe to win the first heart lead, for your jack of hearts would act as a second guard in the suit if the diamond finesse were to lose and North were to gain the lead with the king of diamonds.

If you have to lose the lead twice in order to make the contract, it is often correct to hold up on the first round even if you have *two* tricks in the suit led.

West	East
	(Dummy)
♠ A K 4	♠ 9 6 5
♡ K 9 5	♡ A Q 3
◇ J 10 2	◇ Q 9 6 4
♣ A 9 6 5	♣ K 10 2

You are once again in 3NT, and North leads the 3 of spades to his partner's jack. You will clearly have to knock out both the ace and king of diamonds in order to develop a ninth trick, and the danger is that you will lose three spades and two diamonds if the adverse spades are divided 5–2. You will improve your chances of success considerably if you duck the first round of spades; if South has one of the diamond honours and only two spades, he will now be unable to return a spade when he wins the first round of diamonds, and North's long spades will no longer be a danger.

One particularly effective kind of hold-up play which the declarer may employ in order to nullify the enemy's long suit occurs on a hand of this kind.

West	East
	(Dummy)
♠ K 9 4	♠ A 7 2
♡ A J 3	♡ 5
◇ Q 9 7 2	◇ K J 10 8 4
♣ A 10 5	♣ K 8 4 3

If North leads the king of hearts against your contract of 3NT, you can force him to switch to another suit by ducking the first round; you can then clear the diamonds in perfect safety, no matter which defender has the ace. This kind of hold-up is known as the Bath Coup.

[63]

Mention of the Bath Coup brings me to the final aspect of declarer's all-important play at the first trick: that of how best to play to the trick in order to turn the lead to your advantage. There are, in fact, many suit combinations from which the declarer will make an extra trick if the opponents lead the suit first, his advantage stemming from the fact that he is the last to play to the trick and can therefore select his card accordingly. Generally speaking, the declarer will derive most advantage from having the suit led for him by playing low from the second hand, and you have only to strengthen dummy's heart holding slightly in the last example to find a case where the defence will definitely sacrifice a trick if they lead the suit.

West	East
	(Dummy)
♠ K 9 4	♠ A 7 2
♡ A J 3	♡ 10 5
♢ Q 9 7 2	♢ K J 10 4
♣ A 10 5	♣ K 8 4 3

If North leads the king of hearts against 3NT on this deal, you no longer need to employ a Bath Coup in an attempt to nullify the opponents' suit: you simply win the first trick in order to ensure that you make two heart tricks and the contract. Similarly, of course, if North leads a small heart on the above hand, you are bound to make two heart tricks if you play low from dummy and beat whatever South plays.

However, there are a number of exceptions to this general rule that the declarer should play low from the second hand. In certain situations, you must play a high card from dummy in the hope that you will thereby gain either a trick or at least a vital tempo. This obviously applies if you have Q–x in dummy opposite A–x–x, or J–x opposite A–K–x, when you must play dummy's honour in the hope of sneaking an extra trick; it may also be important on this kind of hand:

West	East
	(Dummy)
♠ K 7 5	♠ J 6
♡ Q 10 8	♡ A K 7
◇ A 9 6 4	◇ Q J 10 5
♣ K 8 2	♣ A 9 5 3

If North leads a small spade against 3NT, it looks as though you will need either a successful diamond finesse or a 4–4 spade break in order to make your contract. There is, however, one additional chance. Play the jack of spades from dummy; if North has led from the ace–queen of spades, the jack will hold the first trick and you will be able to take the diamond finesse in complete safety. If the worst happens and the queen of diamonds loses to North's king, your king of spades will still be safe from attack.

Finally, a situation in which you must play a high card from dummy in order to avoid an unpleasant guess later.

West	(East
	Dummy)
♠ K 7 4	♠ Q 10 5
♡ K Q 9 5	♡ A 8
◇ 10 9 6 3	◇ Q J 8 4
♣ A 6	♣ K J 7 2

If North leads the 3 of spades against your contract of 3NT, you should play the 10 from dummy on the first round in order to smoke out the jack and to avoid being faced with an awkward decision later; if you play a small spade from dummy at the first trick, South will probably insert the 8 or 9 and you will not know whether to play him for the jack or the ace the next time spades are led.

8

The Play of a Suit Contract

Generally speaking, the declarer should have more control over the proceedings in a suit contract than in no trumps. This control obviously stems from the possession of a trump suit, and from the advantage of having his side's long suit as trumps, and the declarer must clearly be careful to make the most of this advantage. I am sure you will all have heard the story about the man walking the Embankment because he omitted to draw trumps: my own feeling is that there must be many more out there by the Thames somewhere because they drew trumps when they should not have, for, while it will more often than not be correct to draw the opponents' small trumps so that they cannot be used for ruffing purposes, there are a number of considerations which should persuade you to postpone matters a little. I propose in this chapter to consider some of the situations in which it is definitely incorrect to start off by drawing trumps.

Possibly the most obvious situation is one in which it is essential to ruff one or two of your losers in dummy.

West	East
	(Dummy)
♠ A 7 5 3	♠ 8 6 4
♡ A K J 9 6 3	♡ Q 10 7
◇ 8 4	◇ A Q 7
♣ A	♣ 10 8 6 4

Suppose that you are West, the declarer in the very good contract of 4♡, and that North leads the king of clubs. As always, you should start by counting your tricks, and you will find that you have nine certain ones: six hearts in your own hand and three outside aces. The vital tenth trick might come from a successful diamond finesse, or you might be lucky enough to find a 3–3 spade break and be able to establish your long spade. However, by far the safest way of ensuring the contract is to ruff your fourth spade with one of dummy's high trumps, and your first move after winning the ace of clubs should be to cash the ace of spades and duck a spade; by conceding your two inevitable spade losers at an early stage, you will eventually be able to ruff your last spade in dummy and make the contract even if the spades break 4–2 and the diamond finesse is wrong. Notice that it would be a mistake to draw even *one* round of trumps before tackling spades: if you do, the defenders might be able to thwart your plan by returning a trump each time they get in with spades.

Another common reason for not drawing trumps immediately is that there is not a great hurry and that something far more urgent has to be done first; for example, there may be an inevitable trump loser and a potential loser in another suit which has to be disposed of first.

	West		East
			(Dummy)
♠	A K 6	♠	8 5 2
♡	K Q 9 8 5	♡	J 10 7 4
♢	9 3	♢	A Q J
♣	K J 7	♣	Q 8 4

If North leads the queen of spades against your contract of 4♡, you should have no difficulty in counting enough tricks for your game: given time, you should come to two spades, four hearts, two clubs and at least two diamonds. However, it is always important to check on your losers as well as your winners, particularly in a suit contract; the danger is that the diamond finesse will lose, in which case you will find yourself faced with three certain losers, with a fourth one looming in the spade suit. It is therefore important to take the diamond finesse *before* attempting to draw trumps; then, if the king of diamonds is wrong and the opponents knock out your second spade trick, you will still be able to discard your losing spade on dummy's third diamond before driving out the ace of hearts. If you make the mistake of tackling trumps at trick two, the opponents will immediately establish their spade trick and you will be in grave danger of going down if the diamond finesse loses.

The advantages of playing a hand in a suit contract rather than in no trumps will be most obvious if you are able to make all or most of your trumps separately. Such a play is called in bridge language a 'cross-ruff', and it is often the correct line to adopt if both your hand and dummy contain an extremely short suit.

West	East (Dummy)
♠ 6	♠ A J 7 2
♡ A 10 8 3	♡ 7
◇ A J 10 9 8	◇ K Q 5 4
♣ 8 6 4	♣ A K 7 2

Suppose that South has opened with a weak 2♠ on this deal and that, as so often happens after a pre-emptive bid by the opponents, your partner has bid a little too much and pushed you into a contract of 6◇. North leads a small trump and, when you count your tricks, you find that there are only four tricks in the three side suits. As there is very little chance of developing any more, your only real chance of success is to make the necessary eight extra tricks from the trump suit, and this you can do by way of a cross-ruff. Provided that you are able to cash the ace of spades without its being ruffed and are able to ruff the second round of hearts low in dummy without suffering an over-ruff, this plan will succeed with little difficulty: you win the trump lead in hand and play to ruff your three losing hearts in dummy, crossing back to hand each time by ruffing spades with high trumps.

If you are planning to execute a cross-ruff of this kind, it is essential to cash all your side-suit winners before embarking on your campaign of ruffs: it might otherwise be possible for one of the opponents to obtain a vital discard or two while you are cross-ruffing, and he will then be able to step in with a small trump when you eventually get around to playing off your aces and kings. To illustrate this important point, look again at this last hand. The bidding indicates that North is short of spades, and he will therefore probably be in a position to discard two or three clubs while you are ruffing spades in your own hand. This means that you must cash the ace and king of clubs at an early stage, while you still can.

A cross-ruff performed entirely with master trumps is called a high cross-ruff, and is clearly the most efficient variety of the play. On most hands, however, you cannot afford to ruff high until you have used all your small trumps. For example, while the last hand almost constituted a high cross-ruff, you had to take the slight risk of ruffing the first heart with a small diamond before you could enjoy the luxury of using only master trumps. Just to make things more complicated, there are certain hands on which the normal procedure is reversed and the declarer ruffs with high trumps first to avoid suffering an over-ruff.

West	East
	(Dummy)
♠ Q J 8 3	♠ A K 9 2
♡ A Q 8 4 2	♡ 6
◇ 8	◇ A J 7 6 4
♣ Q 7 4	♣ J 10 5

You are the declarer in 4♠ after North has opened the bidding with 1♡. North begins with the friendly defence of ace, king and a third club, and your queen holds the third trick. As you now have three tricks in the side suits, you only need seven trump tricks for your contract and the safest line of play is a partial high cross-ruff. After winning the queen of clubs, cash the ace of hearts and ruff a heart low; then cash the ace of diamonds and ruff a diamond low. If these two small ruffs both succeed, you can proceed by cross-ruffing in the red suits with the four top trump honours until you reach a two-card end position in which you have the 9 of spades in dummy and the 8 of spades in your own hand and are certain to make a tenth trick. This line of play avoids the risk of either opponent over-ruffing earlier with the 10 of spades and spoiling your plan by returning a trump.

Another reason for not drawing trumps immediately might be that you have to use dummy's trumps as entries, possibly to dummy's long suit.

West	East
	(Dummy)
♠ K Q J 8 4	♠ A 7 3
♡ K 7 6 5	♡ J 4
♢ A 3	♢ K J 9 7 5 4
♣ 10 7	♣ Q 8

Suppose that you are the declarer in 4♠ and that North cashes two top clubs before switching to a small trump. There is no longer any possibility of playing to ruff two hearts in dummy, and the only real chance of ten tricks now lies in establishing dummy's diamonds. This involves using the ace of trumps as an eventual entry for the long diamonds, assuming that all goes well, and you must clearly get to work on the diamond suit *before* drawing trumps. Win the trump switch in hand and play the ace, king and a third diamond; if you are fortunate enough to find both the spades and the diamonds breaking 3–2, this line of play will land your contract. If the queen of diamonds appears on your right on the third round, of course, you will have to ruff with an honour; you must rely on the spades dividing 3–2 in any case, so that you can draw trumps in two more rounds and end up in dummy with the ace of spades to enjoy the three established diamond tricks.

The last hand was probably fairly straightforward. The situation will be rather more difficult if dummy's trumps have to be used as entries *while* you are establishing dummy's long suit.

West	East
	(Dummy)
♠ J 8	♠ Q 6
♡ A K Q 5 4 3 2	♡ J 10 9
♢ A 10 6	♢ 9 7 5
♣ 7	♣ A 9 8 6 3

Suppose that you are the declarer in the optimistic contract of 4♥ and that North cashes the two top spades and switches to the queen of diamonds. You can count nine top tricks, and the only hope of developing a tenth lies in the club suit: if the opponents' clubs are divided 4–3, you will be able to establish dummy's fifth club by ruffing, but only if you use all dummy's trumps as entries. Win the ace of diamonds and play the ace of clubs and ruff a club. Now cross to dummy with a trump and ruff a club high, cross to dummy with a second trump and ruff another club high. If both opponents follow to the fourth round of clubs, you can now enter dummy with the 9 of hearts to cash the established club for your tenth trick.

It is sometimes important not to draw all the outstanding trumps so that one of dummy's trumps can keep control of a weak side suit.

West	East
	(Dummy)
♠ J 6	♠ A 7
♡ K Q 10 7 6	♡ A J 9
◇ Q 8	◇ K J 10 6 4
♣ A 8 4 2	♣ 7 5 3

Suppose that North leads the king of clubs against your contract of 4♥. There are clearly more than enough tricks for your contract, but it might well be fatal to draw trumps before driving out the ace of diamonds, for this might allow the defence to cash three club tricks when they gain the lead. The solution is to draw only *two* rounds of trumps before embarking on the diamonds, so that dummy's third trump will be a protection against the fourth round of clubs.

Another less common reason for not drawing all the outstanding trumps is that one or two are required in dummy to maintain what is called 'trump control'. You will often find that defenders attempt to gain control of the hand by forcing you to ruff too often in the long trump hand; since it will not usually help their cause to force the short trump hand to ruff, the best counter to a forcing game is often to refuse to ruff until the short trump hand can take the strain.

West	East
	(Dummy)
♠ A	♠ 9 7 5
♡ A Q J 10 4	♡ K 9
◇ A 7 6 5	◇ 10 9 8 4
♣ 9 6 2	♣ A K 7 3

3NT is ice-cold on these hands, but suppose that you find yourself in the inferior contract of 4♡ and that North leads the king of spades. You have nine top tricks and your best chance of a tenth clearly lies in establishing a long diamond if the suit breaks 3–2. You therefore win the ace of spades and immediately play the ace and another diamond, and both opponents follow twice. North wins the second diamond and leads another spade, and you ruff and lead a third diamond to drive out the remaining honour. If the defenders return a third spade at this point, you must refuse to ruff, discarding the club loser from your own hand. Now that you can ruff any further spade lead in dummy, you can no longer be defeated unless there is a very bad trump break. Notice that if you make the mistake of drawing trumps before playing on diamonds, you will be defeated by the likely 4–2 trump break. The defenders will be able to lead spades twice more and, now that you can no longer take the second force in dummy, you will lose control of the hand.

On this last hand, you were able to discard a loser on the third round of spades; no one minds doing this, but it is sometimes essential to discard a *winner* to avoid being forced.

West	East
	(Dummy)
♠ 8	♠ J 7 4
♡ A Q J 10 4	♡ K 9
◇ A K Q	◇ 8 6 4 2
♣ J 10 9 3	♣ A Q 7 5

5♣ is a comfortable contract on these hands; in fact, 6♣ depends on little more than a successful club finesse. However, suppose that you are in the precarious contract of 4♡ and that North leads the king and another spade, which you ruff. You should clearly not attempt to draw trumps at this point, for if it takes four rounds to extract them, you will then be defeated if the club finesse loses. The correct play is to take the club finesse first. If it loses and South returns another spade, you will now have to discard one of your minor-suit winners, leaving dummy in a position to ruff the next round if the defenders persevere with a fourth spade. If you ruff the third spade, reducing your trumps to three, you will lose control of the hand if you attempt to draw trumps and find that the hearts break 4–2.

One final thought about not drawing trumps too quickly: always make sure that it would not pay you to test an important side suit first.

	West		East
			(Dummy)
♠	A K Q 10 4	♠	7 6 5
♡	K Q 8 2	♡	A 7 3
◇	A 8 5	◇	J 7 6
♣	5	♣	J 8 7 6

You are the declarer in 4♠ and you ruff the second round of clubs. Assuming the trumps break reasonably, the contract seems to depend on a 3–3 heart break; however, you can improve your chances considerably by not drawing all the out-standing trumps before testing the important side suit. Draw *two* rounds of trumps and then play the king and ace of hearts and a third heart towards the queen. If the hearts are revealed to be 3–3, all will be well; and, if one of the opponents discards on the third round of hearts, there is an extra chance that the hand with the short hearts also has a doubleton spade, in which case it will be possible to ruff the fourth heart in dummy without suffering an over-ruff.

Even if the hand with the short hearts also has a third trump, no harm will be done. If South has the doubleton heart, he cannot ruff the third round without effectively ruffing thin air and allowing you to discard one of dummy's diamond losers on the queen of hearts. And if the worst comes to the worst and North ruffs the queen of hearts with the last trump, you were doomed to defeat in any case and you will still be able to ruff your last heart in dummy to restrict your losses to one off.

9

The Play of a
Slam Contract

In theory, the only difference between playing a slam contract and playing a part-score or game is that you have to make more tricks. Furthermore, the fact that you can only afford to lose one trick at the most will generally mean that fewer lines of play are open to you in a slam contract and that you should therefore have less difficulty in drawing up your plan of campaign. This is in theory. In practice, of course, there is always a general air of tension at the table when a slam has been bid, probably because of the huge number of points at stake, and the result is that playing a slam never seems to be quite as easy as it perhaps should be. For this reason, I have devoted this chapter entirely to the play of slam contracts, taking the opportunity to discuss any interesting bidding points which happen to arise.

Let us start by considering the play of no trump slams. Similar lines of play are available to the declarer in 6NT or 7NT as in 1NT or 3NT, although there is obviously a limit to the number of times he can hold up. For example, there are hands on which a straightforward finesse is the correct play in a no trump slam.

West	East
	(Dummy)
♠ K 4	♠ A Q J 7
♡ A J 10 3	♡ 7 5 4
◇ A K J 6 4	◇ 8 3
♣ 9 5	♣ A K Q J

There is not much to the bidding of this hand. East opens 1♣, and the 16 high-card points and good diamond suit make the West hand well worth a game-forcing jump to 2◇. Partner rebids 2♠ and, when West now describes the nature of his hand with a waiting bid of 2NT, East is happy to make the natural raise to 6NT.

North leads the 10 of spades and, just as in any contract at any level, your first task should be to count your tricks. You will find that you have eleven certain tricks, and the twelfth can clearly come from either hearts or diamonds. Let us first consider your chances of success if you take an immediate diamond finesse. This will obviously give you twelve tricks straight away if South has the queen and, even if the jack finesse loses, there is still a reasonable chance that the suit will break 3–3 and that your long diamonds will be established. Since the chance of a 3–3 break is slightly over one in three (to be precise, 36%), this means that to play on diamonds will produce twelve tricks just over two-thirds of the time. For those of you who tend to look on percentages in bridge as one of the world's greatest mysteries, I should perhaps explain how I arrive at this figure of two-thirds. The diamond finesse will obviously succeed exactly half the time; of the 50 times in 100 when it loses, the suit will still break 3–3 36% of the time. Since 36% of 50 is 18%, this means that the chance of the diamond play being successful is 50% + 18%, a total of 68%.

How does this compare with your chances of developing the vital extra trick in hearts? To finesse the 10 of hearts and, if this loses to North, to follow this by finessing the jack of hearts will be successful unless North has both the king and queen of hearts. If you think about the possible distribution of the two heart honours, you will realize that there is only a one-in-four chance of their both being in the North hand; this means that to take the repeated heart finesse will give you twelve tricks approximately 75% of the time, and that to play on hearts is therefore a superior line of play to the immediate diamond finesse. I do not believe in memorizing tables and tables of figures before sitting down to play bridge; as this hand shows, however, it is important to have a working knowledge of the approximate chances of the various suit breaks, for you will often find this information helpful in guiding you on to the best line of play, particularly in the all-important slam contracts.

As some of you may have noticed, there is an additional

advantage in playing on hearts on this first hand. Let us assume that you win the spade lead with the king and cross to dummy with a second spade in order to finesse the 10 of hearts. If this loses, you are clearly planning to continue by taking another heart finesse, but there is a way in which you can increase your chances of success quite considerably: before taking the second heart finesse, cash the ace and king of diamonds, just in case the queen drops in two rounds. This is obviously not very likely to happen, for on only one in three of all the 4–2 diamond breaks will the queen be in the doubleton holding, but the play is well worth a try. If you play the two top diamonds and nothing happens, of course, you can revert to your original line of play and cross back to dummy with a club to take the second heart finesse.

This principle of combining two or more chances when you are playing a slam contract is obviously a very important one.

West	East
	(Dummy)
♠ A Q	♠ K 7
♡ 10 9 8 7 2	♡ A K J
◊ A Q J 4	◊ K 8 5
♣ A 10	♣ J 9 8 5 3

Once again you, West, end up in a contract of 6NT, and North leads the jack of spades. The duplication in spades is unfortunate, but it is still quite a reasonable slam. Obviously your best chance is to find North with the queen and not more than two other hearts, in which case a successful finesse of dummy's jack of hearts will produce twelve tricks by way of two spades, five hearts, four diamonds and the ace of clubs. But can you see any way of increasing your chances of success? The only other suit in which you have any hope at all of developing extra tricks is clubs, and leading a small club to the 10 at an early stage will bring in four club tricks if South happens to have a singleton or doubleton honour, or even K–Q–x. The correct play is therefore to win the first spade in dummy and, before testing the hearts, finesse the 10 of clubs. If this loses to North, you can win the return and cash the ace of clubs, just in case the remaining honour drops from either hand to give you four club tricks and the contract. If the club suit does not lie favourably, of course, you will have to fall back on the heart finesse and hope to find the queen of hearts in the North hand. The important point about this hand is that, in order to give yourself every possible chance of making the contract, you must finesse the 10 of clubs *before* trying the hearts; if you take the heart finesse first and it loses, it will be too late to take advantage of a favourable distribution of the club suit.

This principle of combining all the possible chances is such an important one that I would like to show you another hand with the same theme.

West	East (Dummy)
♠ K 8	♠ A Q 4 3
♡ 9 5 4 2	♡ A K 6
◇ A J 8 3	◇ K Q 10
♣ 4 3 2	♣ A K J

West has a slightly awkward bid when his partner opens 2♣. The best response is probably 2NT, which suggests a balanced hand and 8 or 9 points, and East can really do little else but raise to 6NT immediately. North leads the jack of spades, and you find that you have eleven certain tricks in the two hands. The two possible sources of the vital extra trick are a successful club finesse and a 3–3 heart break, which will enable you to duck a round of hearts and then make the long heart in your hand. Once again it is important to plan the play in such a way that you will be able to take advantage of both these possibilities. The correct play is to take jack of spades lead with your king and immediately play a small heart from both hands. You can then win the next lead and test the heart suit by cashing the ace and king. If all goes according to plan and the suit breaks 3–3, your 9 of hearts will become the twelfth trick. If, as is more likely, the adverse hearts are divided 4–2, nothing will be lost and you can still fall back on the club finesse later in the hand. Notice once again the importance of doing things in the right order: if you take the club finesse first and the jack loses to the queen, you will no longer be able to duck a heart and hope for a 3–3 heart break.

If you look again at the club suit on this last hand and at the heart suit on the hand before, you will see that on each occasion you were simply missing the queen and were planning to finesse the jack in the hope of finding the queen favourably situated. As I expect you will all know, you can improve your chances of success just slightly in this kind of situation by cashing one of the top honours *before* finessing the jack; once in a while, this will drop the singleton queen from the right and, since you will still be able to take the straightforward finesse on the next round if the queen fails to appear, playing the ace first can only improve your chances. It is, in fact, a form of safety play, and you should always look out for plays of this kind when you are at the wheel in a slam contract.

West	East
	(Dummy)
♠ A K J 4	♠ 7 5
♡ A K 10 7	♡ 4
◇ 8 6	◇ A K J 5 4 3 2
♣ A Q 7	♣ 8 6 5

You have a difficult opening bid on the West hand. The diamond holding is far from ideal for 2NT, but it is impossible to find a more descriptive opening bid on a balanced hand containing 21 points. East is justified in thinking in terms of a slam in view of his tremendous playing strength and, so that the opening lead should come into the strong hand, rather than through it, he decides to bid 6NT rather than 6◇. In a sense, his fears about the opening lead are vindicated when North leads a small club to the jack and your queen. How would you continue in order to give yourself the best chance of making your contract?

After the original club lead, you have six certain tricks in your own hand, and you only need to make six of dummy's diamonds in order to make the contract. It is tempting to lead a diamond at trick two and to preserve your communications by finessing dummy's jack, but there is one serious snag to this line of play:

if South shows out on the first diamond, you will still have an inevitable diamond loser and it will no longer be possible to make more than three tricks from dummy's long suit. The safety play on this hand is to play a small diamond from both hands at the second trick. Once North follows to the first diamond, in fact, this line of play guarantees the contract no matter where the three remaining diamonds are: even if South is revealed to be void in the suit, you will still be able to finesse the jack of diamonds on the second round to pick up North's queen and collect six diamond tricks.

The safety play in diamonds described in connection with this hand was not a completely perfect one, for there is no way of avoiding losing two tricks in the suit if it is North who turns out to be void. Some safety plays, however, are 100% perfect, in that they can guarantee success no matter how the missing cards are distributed.

West	East
	(Dummy)
♠ A Q 7	♠ K J 6
♡ Q 10 4	♡ A J 5
◇ K J 5 4	◇ A 9 3 2
♣ A 10 6	♣ K Q 8

Once again you are West, the declarer in 6NT, and North leads the 10 of spades. Since you will need to develop at least one extra heart trick in any case, you should test the suit by leading the queen of hearts at the second trick. If this loses to South's king, you will know that you have to play for all four diamond tricks; you should, in fact, play for South to hold Q, Q–x or Q–x–x of diamonds and take an immediate finesse of the jack. Notice that, in this situation, it would be a mistake to cash the ace of diamonds first: it is not going to help to find North with the singleton queen and, just in case South has the bare queen, it is vital to keep the A–9 in dummy to pick up North's 10.

But now suppose that North covers with the king when you lead the queen of hearts at trick two. Now that you have three heart tricks to add to three spades and three clubs, you clearly only need to make three diamond tricks for your contract, and there is a safety play which will guarantee three tricks no matter how the full suit is distributed. Cash the king of diamonds and lead low towards dummy, intending to insert the 9 if North follows with a small card. As you will see if you think about all the possible distributions, this line of play will give you at least three diamond tricks no matter what happens, and this can be described as a perfect safety play.

All the plays which I have described so far in relation to no trump slams can be applied with equal success to suit slams. There are, of course, certain additional plays which are available only in a suit contract, and this is why you should always investigate every possible suit fit when your hand is clearly in the slam zone.

West	East (Dummy)
♠ A Q J 6	♠ 9 3
♡ A 4	♡ 8 7
◇ 9	◇ A Q J 10 8
♣ K Q J 9 6 4	♣ A 10 7 3

This is not an easy slam to bid. You open 1♣ on the West hand, partner bids 1◇, and you rebid 1♠. When partner now gives jump preference to 3♣, your hand becomes very powerful and you should try to find out a little more about the opposite hand by bidding 3♡, the fourth suit. East will interpret this as a try for game at this stage and, in view of his two aces and excellent diamond suit, he will probably jump to 5♣: the knowledge that he has extra values will now enable you to go on to 6♣ with confidence. North leads the king of hearts to your ace. Looking at the two hands, the enormous advantage of playing in a suit contract soon becomes apparent, for it enables you to adopt a line of play which will guarantee the contract against any distribution. After drawing trumps in two rounds, you cross to dummy with the ace of diamonds and lead the queen of diamonds. If South covers with the king, your problems will be over, for you can ruff, discard your losing heart on an established diamond, and eventually take the spade finesse for an overtrick. And if South follows with a small diamond on the queen, you simply discard your losing heart and allow North to win with the king; if he does, it will be the last trick for the defence, for you will now be able to discard three spades on dummy's established diamonds. This type of play, which is obviously only available in a suit contract, is known as a 'Ruffing Finesse'.

The fact that there is a trump suit may also enable you to make your slam contract by means of what is called in bridge language an 'Elimination Play'. It is, in fact, possible to execute a type of Elimination Play in a no trump contract, for there are hands on which you can remove all the safe exit cards from a defender's hand and then throw him in and force him to lead another suit to your advantage. Such situations are always extremely difficult to recognize at the table, however, and the simplest kind of Elimination Play occurs in a suit contract. For example:

West	East (Dummy)
♠ K 7	♠ A 10 3
♡ A J 10 8 3	♡ K Q 9 4
◇ A 8 4	◇ K 7 6
♣ K J 5	♣ A 10 7

The bidding on these hands illustrates an important principle which I referred to in the earlier chapter on slam bidding: that of the advance cue bid. East opens with a strong no trump, and West makes the natural, forcing response of 3♡. With such good trump support and excellent controls, East is too strong for a simple raise to 4♡; he should bid 4♣, which agrees hearts, shows the ace of clubs, and indicates his interest in a slam—all in one bid. West can now cue bid his ace of diamonds in reply, and there should be no difficulty in reaching the excellent contract of six hearts.

In fact, whereas 6NT will depend on a fortunate guess in the club suit, 6♡ depends on nothing more than a 3–1 heart break. North leads the queen of diamonds, and you can win with the ace, draw trumps in three rounds, and play the king, ace and a third spade, ruffing in your hand. The stage is now set for a foolproof endplay. Cash the king of diamonds and exit with the third diamond. No matter which defender wins this trick, he will be forced either to lead a club, thereby locating the vital queen for you, or to concede a fatal ruff and discard in spades or diamonds, enabling you to throw a losing club from one hand while you ruff in the other. Notice that the key to this hand is the elimination play in both spades and diamonds, removing all the safe exit cards from both the defenders' hands before conceding the lead with the third round of diamonds; a perfect elimination of this kind will clearly only be available in a suit contract, and you should always be on the look-out for this type of play when you are at the wheel in a suit slam. Even if you are only able to effect what is known as a 'partial elimination' before you concede an inevitable loser, this in itself will often considerably improve your chances of success.

10

The Opening Lead

The one department of the game in which absolutely no expert player would have the nerve to claim perfection, or indeed anything remotely approaching it, is the opening lead. How often have you heard the defenders wailing 'That would have gone down on a heart lead' or 'A club lead would have beaten 6◇'? Well, you hear exactly the same remarks in the expert game, and a player who could always guarantee to find the best opening lead would be worth his weight in gold in any team.

I do not propose to say very much at this stage about *which* card you should lead from various suit holdings. The accepted standard table of leads is well known, and you will no doubt have made up your mind already on the controversial points which require agreement with your partner: that is, which card you should lead from a worthless three- or four-card holding and what you should lead from a suit headed by the ace and king. I would just like to make one point before going on to consider the more important question of which suit to lead. If you are planning to lead a suit which your partner has bid during the course of the auction, it is important to select the same card as you would if it were an unbid suit. From three or four to an honour, therefore, lead a small card. Many defenders make the mistake of leading their highest card in partner's suit, but it is almost always correct to lead small from holdings like K–x–x and Q–x–x. For one thing, distinguishing between a doubleton honour and three to an honour will enable partner to get a better count of the suit. Secondly, to lead the honour regardless will concede an unnecessary trick in certain situations. For instance, let us suppose that the declarer's holding in partner's suit is one of the three examples given on the following page:

(a)	Dummy	(b)	Dummy	(c)	Dummy
	♣ 7 5		♣ A 5		♣ 7 5
	Declarer		Declarer		Declarer
	♣ Q 8 4		♣ J 8 4		♣ A J 4

If you lead the king of clubs from king to 3 in any of these situations, you will present the declarer with a club trick which he does not deserve and which he will not make if you start off with your lowest club.

Similar considerations apply if your holding in partner's suit is queen to 3. Once again to lead the queen will concede an unnecessary trick if the opposition's holding in the suit is something like:

(d)	Dummy	(e)	Dummy	(f)	Dummy
	♣ 7 5		♣ A 5		♣ K 5
	Declarer		Declarer		Declarer
	♣ K J 4		♣ J 8 4		♣ J 9 4

So much for which card to lead; unfortunately, the choice of which *suit* to lead is rarely as straightforward, and I would like at this stage to run through a number of important general principles which will often enable you to come up with the right answer. Playing against a no trump contract, the defenders will not normally have enough tricks in high cards to defeat the contract. They will therefore need to establish the small cards in their long suits before the declarer has time to drive out the few high-card tricks which he is missing. This is usually a race against time, and the defence must make the most of the advantage of having the first lead. For this reason, it is almost always correct to lead the defenders' long suit against a no trump contract. This normally means that the opening leader kicks off with his own longest suit, but there are certain situations in which he should prefer to lead a suit known or presumed to be held by his partner.

If your partner has bid a suit during the auction, it will generally be correct to lead that suit even if the opponents have ignored the warning and bid strongly in no trumps. In fact,

I would even go further than that: always lead partner's suit unless you have a very good reason not to.

♠ Q 10 7 4 3
♡ 7 5 2
♢ 9 6
♣ K 8 3

If the opponents end up in 3NT after your partner has overcalled in diamonds, forget about your five-card spade suit and lead the 9 of diamonds. Partner clearly has most of the high cards held by the defence, and he may be able to establish his long diamonds even if the declarer has the suit guarded two or three times.

Another situation in which it may be correct not to lead your long suit against a no trump contract is when the suit has been bid in a natural sense by one of the opponents. Unless your holding contains powerful 'middle' cards (for example, something like J–10–9–7–6 or K–10–8–7–6), it will not often prove possible to establish a suit in which one of the opponents is also known to have length. In these circumstances, therefore, it is normally correct to lead an unbid suit in an attempt to find partner's length.

♠ K J 7 4 2
♡ 7 5 3
♢ 10 9 3
♣ A 8

Against a contract of 3NT, you would normally lead the 4 of spades in an attempt to develop your long suit. If the opponents have bid 1♠–2♡–2NT–3NT, however, you are most unlikely to be able to bring your spade suit in, and you should prefer the passive lead of the 10 of diamonds in an attempt to find partner's long suit, and in an attempt to avoid giving declarer an undeserved trick from the lead.

Think twice before leading from length if you have such a poor hand that, even if you are able to establish your long suit, you will almost certainly not be able to regain the lead in order to enjoy it. In these circumstances, it is once again better to lead another unbid suit and try to develop tricks in partner's hand.

♠ 9 8 5
♥ Q 9 6 5 4 2
♦ 10 4
♣ J 3

After the bidding 1NT–3NT, it would almost certainly be a waste of valuable time to attempt to develop this ragged heart suit for, even if partner can help sufficiently for you to be able to establish the long hearts, it is difficult to see how you are going to get in to cash them. Partner is marked with fair values by this auction: help him to develop tricks in his hand by leading the 9 of spades.

Similarly, it may not always be best to lead from your longest suit if it is of poor quality and if you have a strong holding in a shorter suit.

♠ Q J 10 9
♥ 7 5
♦ J 8 6 4 2
♣ K 3

After the bidding 1NT–3NT, there is a strong case for leading the queen of spades rather than your fourth-highest diamond. It will probably take a great deal of effort to develop this ragged diamond suit, and the spade lead has the advantage of developing certain tricks for the defence without the slightest risk of conceding an unnecessary trick to the declarer.

So much for opening leads against no trump contracts, when the defenders are generally attempting to establish long-card tricks. Entirely different considerations apply against a suit contract, when it is usually only the top cards in each suit which are important: the defenders must now attempt to take whatever high-card tricks are due to them while at the same time striving not to present the declarer with anything he does not deserve. The accent in leading against a suit contract is therefore on safety: if this can be combined with aggression, as in the case of a lead from a solid sequence of honours, this is the ideal opening lead.

♠ 7 2
♡ A 10 8 7 5 3
◇ K Q J
♣ 10 4

Whereas you would have an obvious heart lead against a no trump contract, the correct lead after the auction 1♠–3♠–4♠ is the king of diamonds. This develops two potential tricks for the defence immediately, while at the same time being completely safe.

Another aggressive lead which is usually fairly safe is that of a suit bid by partner during the auction. This will apply particularly if partner has made a suit overcall at any stage for, as I tried to emphasize in an earlier chapter, he should rarely overcall in a suit which he does not want you to lead.

There are, of course, occasions on which the bidding absolutely cries out for an attacking lead, even if it involves an element of risk. For example, it may be obvious that dummy has a strong holding in one of the side suits and that the defenders will therefore have to take whatever tricks they can in something of a hurry; in such a case, you may have to choose a slightly dangerous lead from a suit headed by an unsupported honour. There is one very important point which I should like to make in this connection: when considering from which honour holding to make an attacking lead, it is generally correct to choose your shorter suit; that is to say, attack from king to 3 rather than queen to 5.

♠ K 8 3
♡ K 6 4
◇ Q 10 9 8 2
♣ Q 5

If the opponents bid 1♣–1♠–3♣–3♠–4♠, you must realize that your side has to take its tricks in something of a hurry, for dummy has promised a good club suit on which declarer can park his losers. You should therefore attack immediately with the 4 of hearts, hoping to establish and cash two or three heart tricks before it is too late. It is perfectly true, of course, that the sequential honour holding makes a diamond lead much safer than the heart, but you have no time for safety here: this is urgent!

Another attacking lead available to the defence is a lead aimed at obtaining a ruff. A singleton or doubleton lead always stands a fair chance of success for, if you can find partner with a top control either in that suit or in the trump suit, you may well be able to collect a ruff.

♠ A 7 4
♡ Q 8 5 3 2
♢ 6
♣ J 8 7 4

After the bidding 1♠–4♠, the singleton diamond is by far the best lead: your ace of spades means that the declarer will not be able to draw trumps immediately, and the fact that your hand is so weak makes it almost certain that your partner will have a quick entry and that you will be able to collect a ruff or two.

If you have four trumps, or you have every reason to suspect that partner has four, it is generally better to lead from a long suit rather than from a short suit. If you are able to develop a forcing game and compel declarer to ruff your long suit once or twice, he may find it difficult to cope with the bad trump break.

♠ 6
♡ Q 10 8 4 2
♢ 9 8 7 6
♣ A 8 3

If the opponents bid 1♠–2♣–2♠–3♣–4♠, you should realize that partner might well have four trumps. He might therefore be pleased to co-operate in a forcing defence, and the best lead is the 4 of hearts. It seems clear that the opponents have very little to spare for their game contract and a forcing defence, coupled with the bad trump break, may prove a little too much for the unfortunate declarer.

The best lead against a suit contract is often a trump. However, don't fall into the common trap of leading a trump just because you don't know what else to lead: a trump lead should always be designed to achieve a definite purpose, and there are a number of situations in which it may work out very well for the defence.

♠ A J 10 4
♡ 10 4
◇ 8 5 2
♣ Q J 7 3

If the opponents bid 1♠–1NT–2◇–Pass, your left-hand opponent's refusal to return to his partner's first suit makes it almost certain that he is very short in spades. The declarer will therefore be planning to ruff several losing spades in dummy, and you should lead the 2 of diamonds with a view to removing dummy's trumps at every opportunity.

♠ A K 10 4
♡ K Q 7
◇ 8 3
♣ Q 10 6 5

If partner passes your take-out double of 1◇, thereby converting it into a penalty double, he is promising a long and solid holding in trumps. You should therefore lead a diamond originally, in the hope that partner will eventually be able to draw trumps and prevent the declarer from making his small diamonds by ruffing.

♠ Q 10 9 5
♡ 8 3
◇ J 10 7 5
♣ A 5 3

Similarly, if your right-hand opponent's opening bid of 1♡ is passed out, there is a strong case for leading a trump from this hand. Partner is marked with reasonable values on this auction, and his failure to compete at the one level suggests that he has a good holding in the opponents' suit. Once again, therefore, you should try to cut down the declarer's ruffing tricks by leading trumps as often as possible.

♠ A Q 7 5 3
♡ A J 4
◊ K Q 9
♣ 8 3

If your non-vulnerable opponents, who have both bid clubs, sacrifice in 5♣ over your contract of 4♠, there is a good case for doubling and leading a trump. There is clearly no hurry to cash your winners and, as the opponents are likely to be severely lacking in high-card strength in the side suits, they are probably hoping to make as many tricks as possible from their trump suit.

♠ J 10 7 3
♡ Q 7 4
◊ 8 3
♣ Q 10 9 3

If your partner's opening bid of 1NT, showing 15–17 points, is overcalled with 2◊, your best lead is a trump. As you and your partner both have fairly balanced hands, it will obviously be to your advantage to remove the trumps as soon as possible so that the hand can be played on no trump lines.

♠ K J 7
♡ 7 5 2
◊ A J 8 3
♣ J 4 2

After the auction 1♡–3♡–4♡, there is absolutely no clue as to which of those unattractive side suits would make the best opening lead; in fact, any of them could turn out to be beneficial to the declarer, and by far the best lead is a trump.

I would just like to make one more important point in connection with trump leads: unless you have a complete sequence in trumps, always lead the lowest card in the suit. If you hold three small trumps, it is surprising how often your highest card becomes of importance later, especially if the declarer is planning to play the hand on cross-ruff lines.

Similarly, you should lead low from a sequence of honours like J–10–x, for to lead the normal top card may concede an unnecessary trick if partner happens to have a singleton honour in trumps.

So much for which suit to lead when it is left to you to make the decision. There are a number of important situations in which partner doubles the final contract in order to draw your attention to a specific lead, and it is essential to make sure that you know what he has in mind; a mistake by you at that stage will be very expensive, both in terms of points and in terms of partnership confidence.

If partner doubles a freely-bid slam contract, this is generally agreed to be what is known as a 'Lightner' double, calling for an unusual lead. Partner is attempting to draw your attention to the fact that he can probably take a trick or two quickly in an unlikely suit: he might, for example, be able to obtain an immediate ruff in one of the suits bid by the opponents, or he might have two top tricks to cash in one of their suits and judge that it is vital to take them immediately. It is difficult to give you a simple set of rules as to which suit to lead in response to a Lightner Slam Double, for you may have to decide for yourself by reference to your own holdings in the 'unusual' suits.

♠ J 10
♡ 7 3
♢ 9 7 6 5 4 2
♣ Q J 9

Let us suppose that the opponents have reached 6♡ after the sequence 1♢–2♡–2♠–3♡–4♡–6♡. If your partner doubles the final contract, you should lead a diamond; his double calls for an unusual lead and, judging from your length in diamonds, it looks as if he might be able to ruff the first round and cash another certain trick in order to defeat the contract.

A double of a freely-bid 3NT contract also carries with it a suggestion concerning the opening lead. If your side has bid a suit during the auction, the double calls for the lead of that suit.

♠ Q J 10
♡ K J 5 4 2
◇ A 4
♣ 7 4 3

If your right-hand opponent reaches 3NT after you have overcalled his opening bid of 1♣ with 1♡, there is a good case for making the safe lead of a spade rather than risking a lead from your ragged heart suit. If partner doubles the final contract, however, you must lead a heart: his double suggests that he can offer some assistance in your suit.

If the defenders have bid *two* suits during the auction, a double of 3NT by partner suggests that you should lead your suit rather than his.

♠ K J 7 4 3
♡ 9 5
◇ A 10 9 5
♣ 10 4

Suppose that the auction starts 1♣ on your right, 1♠ from you, 2◇ on your left, and 2♡ from partner. If the opponents now push on to 3NT and your partner doubles, the suggestion is that you should lead a spade rather than a heart.

Finally, if the opponents have reached 3NT after an uninterrupted auction, a double calls for the lead of dummy's first-bid suit.

♠ 7 5 4
♡ 8 3
◇ Q 10 8 6 4
♣ A 9 2

If the opponents bid 1♡–2NT–3NT, you would normally make the natural lead of the 6 of diamonds. If partner doubles the final contract, however, you should lead the 8 of hearts; his double shows a powerful holding in the suit bid by dummy.

I I

Defence

The fundamental principle of defence which I always try to emphasize to inexperienced players is: 'Don't get busy unless you really have to'. A surprisingly high proportion of contracts are doomed to defeat right from the start, either because the adverse cards are poorly placed for the declarer, because the important suits are breaking badly for him, or because the declaring side has done a little too much in the bidding. If this is the case, it is important for the defenders to adopt a purely passive role, concentrating entirely on not opening up new suits to the declarer's advantage and on not giving the declarer any tricks which are not his by right.

It has been estimated that, on average, defenders concede half a trick every time they switch to a new suit, and this proposition once again emphasizes the importance of their going passive as often as they possibly can. The trouble is, of course, that it is not always easy for the defenders to decide whether or not they can afford to relax, and one of the special qualities distinguishing a good defender from the rest is his ability to judge just when it is vital to throw caution to the winds and get busy. I hope in this chapter to suggest a number of situations in which an active defence is required.

The third player sometimes has to be on his toes to help his partner to develop and cash his long suit against a no trump contract. For example, he may need to unblock a high card in situations like the one on the following page:

```
                    North
                    A 7 4
West                            East
Q J 10 6 3                      K 2
                    South
                    9 8 5
```

West leads the queen and, whether or not declarer plays the ace from dummy, East must play the king. If he fails to unblock, he will be compelled to win the second round of the suit with the king and the defenders will be unable to make any further progress.

A more difficult case:

```
                    North
                    Q 6
West                            East
A 10 7 5 4 3                    J 8
                    South
                    K 9 2
```

West leads the 5 against a no trump contract and declarer plays the queen from dummy. East must play the jack under the queen and hope that he can gain the lead before it is too late. If he fails to get out of the way at trick one, he will be allowed to hold the jack on the second round and the defenders will no longer be able to run the suit.

The third player may also have to think quickly at trick one in cases where he needs to finesse against his partner.

```
                    North
                    7 5
West                            East
Q 9 8 4 2                       A J 3
                    South
                    K 10 6
```

It is very rarely correct play to finesse against your partner, and the normal defence on this holding would be for East to go up with the ace and return the jack. If it seems unlikely that

West has a side-suit entry, however, East does best to play the
jack at trick one and winkle out declarer's king. If the ace
appears on the first round, South will withhold his king until the
third round and West's long suit will be immobilized.

Later in the play, the third player may need to take active
steps in order to preserve his partner's entry. For example:

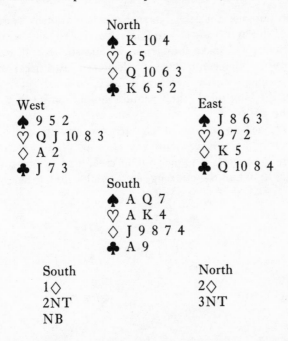

North
♠ K 10 4
♡ 6 5
♢ Q 10 6 3
♣ K 6 5 2

West
♠ 9 5 2
♡ Q J 10 8 3
♢ A 2
♣ J 7 3

East
♠ J 8 6 3
♡ 9 7 2
♢ K 5
♣ Q 10 8 4

South
♠ A Q 7
♡ A K 4
♢ J 9 8 7 4
♣ A 9

South	North
1♢	2♢
2NT	3NT
NB	

West leads the queen of hearts against 3NT. Declarer wins
with the king, crosses to dummy with the king of spades, and
leads a low diamond. To defeat the contract, East must go in
with the king of diamonds and return a second heart while his
partner retains his certain entry.

The winning defence against a no trump contract sometimes
involves killing dummy's long suit rather than establishing
partner's. Such a campaign may well call for extremely active
defence, particularly by the second player.

North
A J 10 6 2

West   East
K 8 4   Q 9 3

South
7 5

Let us suppose that the North hand is extremely short of entries. If declarer leads low to the jack and East wins with the queen, South will make four tricks by finessing the 10 on the second round. East can restrict the declarer to two tricks in the suit by ducking the jack. The best defence, however, is for West to insert the king on the first round: this limits South to one trick—the ace.

I mentioned in an earlier chapter the way in which the declarer may be able to employ a hold-up play to nullify a defender's long suit. It is possible in certain situations for the defenders to obtain their revenge by way of a similar tactic.

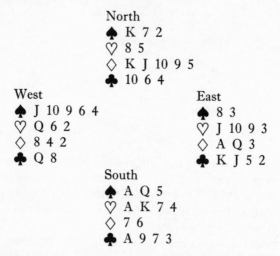

North
♠ K 7 2
♡ 8 5
◇ K J 10 9 5
♣ 10 6 4

West   East
♠ J 10 9 6 4   ♠ 8 3
♡ Q 6 2   ♡ J 10 9 3
◇ 8 4 2   ◇ A Q 3
♣ Q 8   ♣ K J 5 2

South
♠ A Q 5
♡ A K 7 4
◇ 7 6
♣ A 9 7 3

West leads the jack of spades against 3NT and South wins the queen and finesses the jack of diamonds. If East wins with the queen and returns a spade, declarer will be able to go up with the ace and knock out the ace of diamonds while there is still a spade entry in dummy. The winning defence is for East to duck the jack of diamonds. This will effectively kill dummy's long suit, and careful defence should now restrict the declarer to seven tricks.

There are occasions on which a hold-up play by the defence will not succeed because the declarer has sufficient length in dummy's suit. The only defence in these cases may be to launch an all-out assault on dummy's side-suit entry.

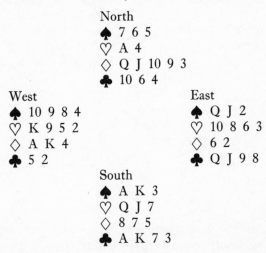

North
♠ 7 6 5
♡ A 4
◇ Q J 10 9 3
♣ 10 6 4

West
♠ 10 9 8 4
♡ K 9 5 2
◇ A K 4
♣ 5 2

East
♠ Q J 2
♡ 10 8 6 3
◇ 6 2
♣ Q J 9 8

South
♠ A K 3
♡ Q J 7
◇ 8 7 5
♣ A K 7 3

West leads the 10 of spades against 3NT and South wins with the king and sets to work on diamonds. West ducks the first round to kill dummy's suit if South has only two diamonds, but it soon becomes clear from East's distributional signals that South has a three-card holding in the suit. This makes the ducking play ineffective, and West has to get busy and remove dummy's entry. After winning the second round of diamonds, he must switch to the king of hearts—the so-called 'Merrimac Coup'. This gives South three heart tricks but it restricts him to one diamond trick and eight tricks in total.

One of the most important principles of good defence is that you should always keep a constant count of the tricks which are available to the declarer. Counting in this way will often ring the alarm bells and indicate that it is time to get busy in defence;

it may be, for example, that a spectacular switch is required to defeat the contract.

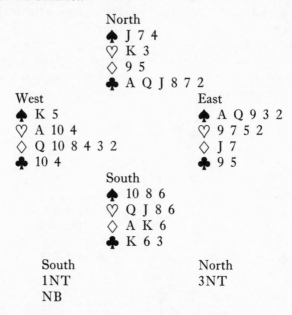

North
♠ J 7 4
♡ K 3
♢ 9 5
♣ A Q J 8 7 2

West
♠ K 5
♡ A 10 4
♢ Q 10 8 4 3 2
♣ 10 4

East
♠ A Q 9 3 2
♡ 9 7 5 2
♢ J 7
♣ 9 5

South
♠ 10 8 6
♡ Q J 8 6
♢ A K 6
♣ K 6 3

South	North
1NT	3NT
NB	

West leads the 4 of diamonds, and East's jack loses to declarer's ace. South now leads a small heart from his hand, and it is time for West to do a little counting. The natural defence seems to be for West to duck the first heart, intending to win the second round and then drive out the king of diamonds while the king of spades remains as an entry. However, the fact that South elected to play a heart at trick two strongly suggests that he has the king of clubs in the closed hand. If this is so, West can count nine tricks for declarer: six clubs, two diamonds and the king of hearts. The only hope of defeating the contract therefore lies in the spade suit, and the correct defence is for West to go up with the ace of hearts and switch to the king and another spade.

There are certain situations in which it is vital for a defender to switch to a precise card in the correct suit. For example, his honour cards may 'surround' a lower honour which is visible in dummy:

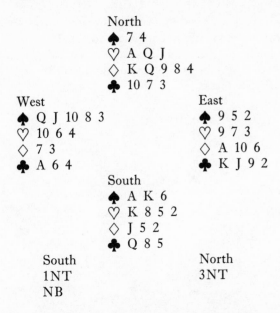

North
♠ 7 4
♡ A Q J
♦ K Q 9 8 4
♣ 10 7 3

West
♠ Q J 10 8 3
♡ 10 6 4
♦ 7 3
♣ A 6 4

East
♠ 9 5 2
♡ 9 7 3
♦ A 10 6
♣ K J 9 2

South
♠ A K 6
♡ K 8 5 2
♦ J 5 2
♣ Q 8 5

South	North
1NT	3NT
NB	

West leads the queen of spades, and South wins with the ace and leads the jack and another diamond, driving out East's ace. East must now pause to count declarer's tricks. If South has the ace of clubs, he must have at least nine tricks by way of two spades, four diamonds, one club and the successful heart finesse. And if South does not have the ace of clubs, he must hold the king of hearts and have at least nine tricks available again. The time has therefore come for East to adopt an active defence, and his only hope is that his partner has the ace of clubs and that the defence can cash four club tricks. A count of South's high-card points makes it clear that he must have at least two points in clubs, and it is therefore essential for East to switch to the *jack* of clubs. On any other defence, South can duck the club switch round to dummy's 10 and give himself a certain stop in the suit.

Most of the defensive plays mentioned are available against suit contracts as well as against no trumps. Furthermore, suit contracts offer additional opportunities for active defence, and many of these involve engineering a ruffing trick or two. In my experience, however, inexperienced defenders are often a little over-anxious to give or collect a ruff. They subsequently realize that one ruff is frequently not sufficient to defeat the contract, and a good defender should always pause to consider what is to happen next. Wherever possible, you should try to organize a ruff for *both* defenders.

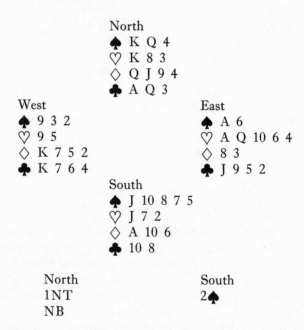

North
♠ K Q 4
♡ K 8 3
◇ Q J 9 4
♣ A Q 3

West
♠ 9 3 2
♡ 9 5
◇ K 7 5 2
♣ K 7 6 4

East
♠ A 6
♡ A Q 10 6 4
◇ 8 3
♣ J 9 5 2

South
♠ J 10 8 7 5
♡ J 7 2
◇ A 10 6
♣ 10 8

North   South
1NT   2♠
NB

West leads the 9 of hearts against 2♠, and East should have little difficulty in recognizing this as a doubleton lead. Before giving his partner a third-round heart ruff, however, East should realize that the contract will not be defeated unless West has either the ace or the king of diamonds. He must therefore switch to a diamond at trick two, so that he can win the ace of spades, give his partner a heart ruff and collect a diamond ruff in return.

Similarly, in the situation depicted at the top of the following page:

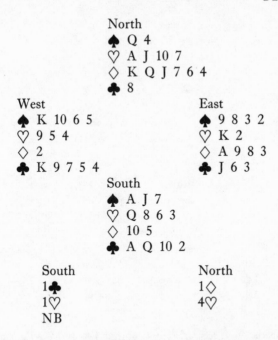

North
♠ Q 4
♡ A J 10 7
◇ K Q J 7 6 4
♣ 8

West
♠ K 10 6 5
♡ 9 5 4
◇ 2
♣ K 9 7 5 4

East
♠ 9 8 3 2
♡ K 2
◇ A 9 8 3
♣ J 6 3

South
♠ A J 7
♡ Q 8 6 3
◇ 10 5
♣ A Q 10 2

South	North
1♣	1◇
1♡	4♡
NB	

West leads the 2 of diamonds, an obvious singleton, and East can count three certain defensive tricks: the ace of diamonds, a diamond ruff and the king of hearts. If he thoughtlessly gives his partner a ruff at trick two, that is the end of the hand for the defence. East should, in fact, pause to consider where his side's fourth trick is going to come from. If West has an ace, of course, there is no problem. However, if he has the king of spades, it is vital for East to switch to a spade *before* giving partner his ruff. Since the bidding makes it almost certain that West has three trumps, it can do no harm to postpone the ruff; the first job to be done is to find and establish the setting trick.

Sometimes the ruffing trick which the defenders manage to engineer arises as a result of a trump promotion play. Such a play often requires an imaginative piece of defence, as exemplified by the strategy employed on the next page:

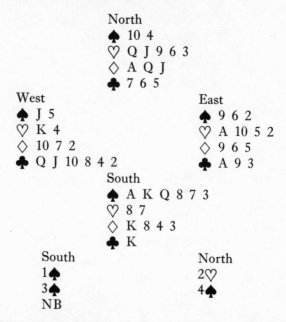

North
♠ 10 4
♡ Q J 9 6 3
♢ A Q J
♣ 7 6 5

West
♠ J 5
♡ K 4
♢ 10 7 2
♣ Q J 10 8 4 2

East
♠ 9 6 2
♡ A 10 5 2
♢ 9 6 5
♣ A 9 3

South
♠ A K Q 8 7 3
♡ 8 7
♢ K 8 4 3
♣ K

South	North
1♠	2♡
3♠	4♠
NB	

West leads the queen of clubs against 4♠ and East's ace fells South's singleton king. The best chance of defeating the contract appears to lie in making two heart tricks and a trump trick. This means that South must have precisely two hearts, for he would probably have chosen to raise his partner's heart bid if he held three-card support. This in turn means that West must also have two hearts and there is therefore an obvious chance of a trump promotion play. After winning with the ace of clubs, East should switch to a small heart. The king, ace and a third heart then establish a certain trump trick for the defenders.

INDEX